CLASSIC FRIENDS

Companions for Our Spiritual Journey

Jerry Flora

CLASSIC FRIENDS

Companions for Our Spiritual Journey

Jerry Flora

Gracednotes Ministries

Gracednotes Ministries
405 Northridge St. NW
North Canton, OH. 44720

Printed in the United States

ISBN 979-83-40949332

Independently Published

CONTENTS

FOREWORD

This book is a surprise. The preface recounts how a fifteen-year-old manuscript was discovered and two friends decided it should be published.

Dr. Judy Reber McLaughlin, one of my graduate assistants at Ashland Theological Seminary, had proofread an earlier book for me and carefully checked all its scripture references. Dr. JoAnn Streeter Shade is well known both as an author and for her work on behalf of many writers, including my wife Julie and me, to bring their ideas to publication.

These two friends have contributed to this book in ways far beyond where their names appear. I can only thank them for their perseverance, hoping that what you read here may inform you or even inspire you. If through our cumulative effort you make some new friends, classic friends, we can only thank God. Soli Deo gloria!

Jerry Flora
All Saints' Day 2024

PREFACE

That this collection of devotional writers would be titled *Classic Friends: Companions for Our Spiritual Journey* is appropriate indeed, for it is out of friendship that the idea of publishing the book came to fruition. Its author, Dr. Jerry Flora, first introduced me to these friends in his History of Devotional Literature course when I was a student at Ashland Theological Seminary in the late 1980s. My circle of friendship continued to expand, as did the books on my library shelves, due to the influence of the Disciplined Order of Christ and my doctoral work in Formative Spirituality at Duquesne University.

Credit also needs to be given to what we learned from the COVID-19 pandemic when we focused on the task of culling as one of our responses to being shut down. We took to our closets and dressers, cabinets, files, bookshelves, basements, attics and garages. We filled our vehicles with donation bags and boxes and, when it was safe, headed to whatever agency in our community accepted what the Quakers called our "cumber." Add to that the challenges of aging well, as becoming an octogenarian in 2023 seemed to energize my desire to continue culling my possessions so that when it is my turn to meet Jesus, the job of dispersing my remaining worldly goods will be easier for my children, family and friends.

And so it was that in the spring of 2024 the manuscript that Dr. Jerry Flora had given me to proofread several years before resurfaced. I reviewed my discovery, which was full of my editing comments and suggestions and, you guessed it, put it back in the file drawer because I remembered that he had decided not to publish it. A few more months would pass by before my friend, JoAnn Streeter Shade, and I scheduled a visit with Jerry and Julie Flora in their Ashland home to discuss our idea of publishing the manuscript. The rest they say is history.

A gifted writer herself, JoAnn has served as a midwife to many authors through Gracednotes Ministries and has done a masterful job in bringing this book to print. It has been a joy to work with her as we continued nurturing our friendship over time and distance. When we meet, we talk about our families, share our concerns for our world and nation and encourage each other to generate gratitude lists that remind us that life is good and we are loved. We trust that *Classic Friends* will continue to nourish us spiritually as each day unfolds. It has been said that friendship is a sheltering tree. We hope that in the reading of *Classic Friends* you will take time to bask in the sunshine of God's friendship and love. *Soli Deo gloria!*

Judy Reber McLaughlin

INTRODUCTION

Come on in. I want you to meet some friends of mine. You already know a few of them by name, but within these pages you will enjoy getting better acquainted. Some of them I have known for a long time – in one case about seventy years. Others are newer, but they are all close personal friends. I learn from them, they support and encourage me, and I have had the privilege of introducing them to other folks like you.

Their words live today in classics of Christian devotion. We have classic movies, classic cars, and even classic jokes. But what makes some devotional books classics?

First of all, they are biblical. They are based on what The Book says, and they reflect the story it tells. They may quote it directly or allude to it indirectly. John Bunyan's *Pilgrim's Progress*, for example, is laced with biblical quotations, but the sayings of the desert Christians are more indirect. Either way, what scripture says about the triune God and human experience in the world is at the heart of their message. Friends don't always agree, and at times I question some of what they say. Invariably, however, they help me to know and love God more and serve my neighbor better.

Another part of what makes these books classics is that they are the fruit of personal experience. Take, for instance, Augustine, the fast-track social climber who gradually inched his way toward God. Or Oswald Chambers, the "irreverent reverend" who was passionately serious about following Christ. Or Julian of Norwich, who interpreted what she saw and heard in a once-in-a-lifetime visionary experience. And what pair could be more different than the simple monk Brother Lawrence and philosophy professor Thomas Kelly, Ph.D.? Yet the two men have a similar message, based on their very different life stories.

They are, in fact, two of my closest friends because I share fragments of their experience.

Third, these books are universally recognized. While we all have our favorite writers, these have found unusually broad appeal. They may not sound like me or you, but in the wisdom of people who are widely read, these are among the best. There must be good reasons, for example, why *The Imitation of Christ* by Thomas à Kempis is the world's best-selling devotional book. When I go to an art gallery and see both ancient and recent works on display, I know that the art is not on trial. I am on trial. The question is, can I appreciate and value what experts recognize as outstanding?

Finally, these books are time-tested. Newer is not always better, whether in wine or in writing. C. S. Lewis noted that our culture practices "chronological snobbery." We look down on anything that is not up to date or in the newest fashion. For healthy balance he recommended reading one old book for every new one that we finish. Or, failing that, an old one for every two new ones. Old is not necessarily better, but when it is combined with the qualities already mentioned, it may mean that we have a classic. True classics are timeless. No matter when they were written, they have a way of speaking to all generations.

I must caution you, however, that this selection is very personal and not fully rounded. Although I have Eastern Orthodox friends, they are not here right now. Also, these particular friends are nearly all from Europe and North America. And, reflecting, the history of the church, men outnumber women in the books represented. Hopefully, in another place and time all these shortcomings can be corrected, and we shall see the wonder of God, in a broader, brighter spectrum.

It has been my privilege to introduce these friends to four different audiences: students at Ashland Theological Seminary, the Christian Heirs class at Ashland's Park Street Brethren Church, the Kairos School of Spiritual Formation in eastern Pennsylvania, and the LifeSpring School of Spiritual Formation in northern Ohio. I dedicate these pages to all of these students with gratitude and affection.

As a practical word regarding the organization of these pages, the chapters are ordered chronologically, ranging from the third to the twentieth century. Each chapter tells a bit about the life story of my friends, and then I've chosen some of their words so that their own voices are heard. Other resources are mentioned in the text and included in the bibliography for further study.

Now it is time for you to meet these friends — just part of the cloud of witnesses to the living God in our world. Come on in. Welcome to the conversation!

1

WILDERNESS WARRIORS

DESERT CHRISTIANS

In the beginning, the followers of Jesus lived precariously. For three hundred years after his death, Roman authorities did not know what to make of them. In some places they seemed to be a sect within Judaism, while elsewhere they appeared to be a new, potentially dangerous religion. Judaism was a known entity with certain legal rights, but an independent Christianity was not. Persecution often hovered on the horizon for those who maintained Jesus is Lord, especially when that conflicted with patriotic rallies where the chant was, "Caesar is Lord."

If persecution did break out, it was usually temporary and local. The first known Roman assault on Christians occurred after a huge summer fire in A.D. 64 destroyed much of the Eternal City. Rumors spread that agents of Emperor Nero had started the blaze, so to divert suspicion, authorities blamed the Christians. Believers in and around Rome were arrested, tortured, and executed by hideous methods. All this was reported a half-century later by the historian Tacitus, who had little sympathy for Nero and even less for Christians. In turn, the Christians maintained that in the slaughter the Romans had crucified Peter and beheaded Paul. But there is no evidence that the persecution spread beyond the capital or lasted any great length of time. Terrible as it was, it mercifully ended.

For two centuries persecutions followed in various places and times, all of them temporary and local. They alternated with longer periods of relative calm when evangelizing flourished and local Christian assemblies grew. Then in the middle of the third century the emperor Decius ordered the first international attack on the new religion. Thankfully that brutal assault lasted only two years, ending with the death of Decius in A.D. 251.

In that same year a baby was born who would later spearhead a new movement among Jesus' followers. Up to that time, following St. Paul's strategy, evangelism had spread the faith from cities to towns and into villages. This new movement was into the desert and the baby who would lead it was Anthony, the pioneer desert monk. He grew up in Alexandria, Egypt, when the Roman Empire was shaking, especially in the West, and no one knew what to expect. In the uncertainty of the time many people sought refuge in whatever the new religion could offer. Church buildings were constructed and filled for worship, but catechetical instruction broke down under weight of the numbers, and bishops faced a faith that was becoming popular.

Persecution still threatened, but the powers in the desert were equally daunting. Anthony took up the challenge and lived as a hermit for twenty years, giving himself to a life of simplicity in solitude. Alone and away, he engaged in spiritual warfare, battling the world, the flesh, and the devil. Then, in response to God's call, he returned to the Egyptian capital where he quickly became a sensation. His piercing discernment and spiritual wisdom intimidated some and attracted others. After five years in the public eye in the city, he returned to the desert where he died at an advanced age in A.D. 356. By then persecution had ended, and Christianity had become a legal religion in the empire. Alexandria's archbishop Athanasius, famous for his defense of orthodoxy, wrote *The Life of St. Anthony*. His biography of the old wilderness warrior probably did more than any other book to popularize the call to monastic life.

It is imperative that we understand the monastic movement because it is the foundation for so much of what followed. "Monastic" comes from the Greek word *monochos,* which means "solitary" or "alone." Like Anthony, the first monks were hermits who lived by themselves not in the Sahara Desert, but in deserted places where they could be alone. Some stayed within walking distance of others so they could worship together on weekends. With the passing of time groups of monks began living together, and the idea of a monastic "house" or community emerged.

The goal of these wilderness warriors was to live a totally committed, highly disciplined life. They were not running or hiding from the real world – they were running to God. They intended to be athletes of the spirit, soldiers of Christ. Some believed that with the Christianizing of the cities and countryside, the demons had retreated into the desert. These warriors were determined to confront them there and defeat them by prayer and fasting, humility and obedience. As precedents for this wilderness life they could cite Moses, who lived forty years as a shepherd before he attempted to lead Israel. Or Elijah who apparently was a hermit but came into town when God gave him a message to deliver. John the Baptizer followed his example, and Jesus often left the cities to seek out solitary places for prayer. Hebrew prophets had even described Israel's wilderness wandering as a time of special nearness to God (Hos. 2:14-15; Jer. 2:1-3; 31:2-3). Thus, the thinking went, if these members of the true Israel moved to the wilderness, they too might find God especially close.

Many of the earliest monks were simple, unlettered men who sought God by faith and fortitude. They lived quietly in their cells (huts or small caves), meditated on scripture, prayed the psalms, and supported themselves by gardening, making baskets, or weaving mats. They became noted for their hospitality, discernment, and non-judgmental attitude toward outsiders. Many people sought them for counsel, often asking, "Father, give me a word." As the movement grew into the thousands, educated individuals – women as well as men – joined their ranks. Standards of conduct and behavior began to surface as monks clustered around natural leaders.

One noted figure was Pambo (d. about 373), an illiterate Egyptian until he learned to read the scriptures. Some of his contemporaries considered him one of the desert's greatest masters. Another was Macarius the Great (d. 390), a former camel driver who visited Anthony's hermitage at least twice. John the Dwarf ranks as one of the most colorful desert characters. In order to preserve his solitude, he dug an underground cave for himself. Disciples preserved many of his sayings, a testimony to his great influence. Moses the Black, a former thief and outlaw, was also a forceful figure. He became a gentle leader of great influence until he and five fellow monks were massacred in the year 405. Evagrius (d. 400) and Arsenius (d. 449) intimidated simpler monks because of their great learning and personal austerity. The former spent ten years as a pupil of Macarius while the latter, after a career in the emperor's palace, placed himself under the guidance of John the Dwarf.

There were also outstanding women, although less has been preserved about them. We know them mostly through the few sayings attributed to them. Sarah, for instance, came from a wealthy Christian family where she received a good education. She served as spiritual leader of a women's monastery until her death near the age of eighty. Several Theodoras are known, the most prominent being a fourth-century colleague of Alexandria's archbishop. Monks often consulted her about monastic life. Syncletica left her respected family and great education to embrace the desert life. Other women gathered around her as she became the best-known of the ancient mothers. Syncletica lived into her eighties and died about A.D. 460 after three years of intense suffering.

Desert monasticism was a feature of the Eastern church. It flourished in the Holy Land as well as in Egypt to the south and Syria to the north. The man who brought its message to the West was John Cassian (360-435), whose lifetime parallels that of Augustine. Born in southeastern Europe, he became a monk in Bethlehem, then a student of the Egyptian ascetics, then a deacon in Constantinople under the great orator-bishop John Chrysostom. When the latter was deposed,

Cassian traveled to Rome to seek help for him. Apparently Cassian remained in Europe, moving eventually to France, where he founded a monastery at Marseilles. His writings, based on his extensive experience with Egypt's desert Christians, brought monasticism from the East into the West. Thanks to him and other anonymous collectors, we have remnants of this significant early movement in the church.

The wisdom of these wilderness warriors, often expressed in terse statements or near-riddles, combined with their ascetic discipline to win the admiration of the church both East and West. From the fifth century on, European Christianity favored monastic life as the highest expression of faith and spirituality. As we shall see in the next chapter, it was the dream of Augustine to retire with a few friends to a country house where they could live a life of prayer and study in a community of love. Monasticism colored all of Western belief and practice for a thousand years. Then about 1520 Martin Luther, a monk himself, began a reformation of the church's thinking. Even now, in our own day, the disciplined devotion of the original desert Christians continues to inspire. A new monasticism is arising, often seeing inner cities as a modern-day desert needing to be captured for Christ.

Voices from the Desert

Sayings of the desert Christians and brief biographies of them appear in the writings of Cassian as well as in anonymous Greek and Latin collections. Translations edited by Oxford scholar Benedicta Ward are among the best. An especially attractive approach is in Thomas Merton's tiny book *The Wisdom of the Desert* (New York: New Directions Publishing Corporation, 1960). In less than one hundred pages the brilliant American monk offers a winsome introduction together with his own translation of sayings from a Latin collection. Here is a representative sampling of their discipline, insight, and humor from their own voices. They may seem rather eccentric, but they remain classic friends.

On the basics: Abbot Pambo questioned Abbot Anthony saying: "What ought I to do?" And the elder replied: "Have no confidence in your own virtuousness. Do not worry about a thing once it has been done. Control your tongue and your belly" (I, p. 25).

On judging: A brother in Scete happened to commit a fault, and the elders assembled, and sent for Abbot Moses to join them. He, however, did not want to come. The priest sent him a message, saying: "Come, the community of the brethren is waiting for you." So he arose and started off. And taking with him a very old basket full of holes, he filled it with sand, and carried it behind him. The elders came out to meet him, and said: "What is this, Father?" The elder replied: "My sins are running out behind me, and I do not see them, and today I come to judge the sins of another!" They, hearing this, said nothing to the brother but pardoned him (XLI, p. 40).

On action: Abbot Pastor said: "If you have a chest full of clothing, and leave it for a long time, the clothing will rot inside it. It is the same with the thoughts in our heart. If we do not carry them out by physical action, after a long while they will spoil and turn bad" (XLVI, p. 42).

On distracting thoughts: A brother came to Abbot Pastor and said: "Many distracting thoughts come into my mind, and I am in danger because of them." Then the elder thrust him out into the open air and said: "Open up the garments upon your chest and catch the wind in them." But he replied: "This I cannot do." So the elder said to him: "If you cannot catch the wind, neither can you prevent distracting thoughts from coming into your head. Your job is to say No to them" (L, p. 43).

On commitment: Abbot Lot came to Abbot Joseph and said: "Father, according as I am able, I keep my little rule, and my little fast, my prayer, meditation and contemplative silence; and according as I am able I strive to cleanse my heart of thoughts: now what more should I do?" The elder rose up in reply and stretched out his hands to heaven, and his fingers became like ten lamps of fire. He said: "Why not be totally changed into fire" (LXXII, p. 50).

On tears: Abbess Syncletica of holy memory said: "… A man who wants to light a fire first is plagued by smoke, and the smoke drives him to tears, yet finally he gets the fire that he wants. So also it is written: Our God is a consuming fire. Hence we ought to light the divine fire in ourselves with labour and with tears" (LXXXIX, p. 55).

On self-awareness: Abbot Joseph asked Abbot Pastor: "Tell me how I can become a monk." The elder replied: "If you want to have rest here in this life and also in the next, in every conflict with another say: 'Who am I?' And judge no one" (CV, p. 63).

On relaxing: Once Abbot Anthony was conversing with some brethren, and a hunter who was after game in the wilderness came upon them. He saw Abbot Anthony and the brothers enjoying themselves, and disapproved. Abbot Anthony said: "Put an arrow in your bow and shoot it." This he did. "Now shoot another," said the elder. "And another, and another." The hunter said: "If I bend my bow all the time it will break." Abbot Anthony replied: "So it is also in the work of God. If we push ourselves beyond measure, the brethren will soon collapse. It is right, therefore, from time to time, to relax their efforts" (CVI, p. 63).

On quarreling: There were two elders living together in a cell, and they had never had so much as one quarrel with one another. One therefore said to the other: "Come on, let us have at least one quarrel, like other men." The other said: "I don't know how to start a quarrel." The first said: "I will take this brick and place it here between us. Then I will say: 'It is mine.' After that you will say: 'It is mine.' This is what leads to a dispute and a fight." So then they placed the brick between them, one said: "It is mine," and the other replied to the first: "I do believe that it is mine." The first one said again: "It is not yours, it is mine." So the other answered: "Well then, if it is yours, take it!" Thus they did not manage after all to get into a quarrel (CXII, p. 67).

I am grateful for these voices that still echo from the deserts of the early centuries of Christianity, even when the identity of these early followers is not fully known. Our next friend, Augustine of Hippo, comes to us from the same era of history. Much better known than the desert monks, he too had a profound impact on the early church

2

PASSIONATE, ELOQUENT AFRICAN

AUGUSTINE OF HIPPO

What do you do if you are a Christian mother, and your teenage son turns out to be both a sensitive genius and a sexual explorer? Especially if he rejects the faith you have worked so hard to teach him? That was the dilemma Monica faced in the ancient North African town of Thagaste, today in Algeria. She and her husband Patricius (Patrick) were the parents of a brilliant, strong-willed son they named Aurelius Augustine. Born in A.D. 354, near the year of Anthony's death, he lived at the time when the desert Christians were moving into their heyday. Some experts consider him the most influential figure in Western Christianity since the apostles. His ideas guided the church – for better or worse – through a thousand years after his death, and many leaders of the Protestant Reformation followed Augustine in their thinking.

Patricius and Monica did not agree on their goals. She was a devout Christian while he was, nominally at least, a pagan. Her greatest pleasure would be to see her son fully committed in Christian faith and a leader in the church. Patricius' greatest joy would be to see Augustine the father of a fine family and a leader in public life. They started their bright boy in the local schools, but he hated to study languages, and classroom discipline was brutal, as beatings for wrong answers were common. When he was about sixteen they sent him on to Carthage,

North Africa's greatest city, where more opportunities awaited – opportunities to stray as well as study.

Augustine's sexual drive fascinated him, and he actively sought its fulfillment. He and one of the local girls began living together, and they had a son whom they named Adeodatus (God-given). We don't know the name of the girl, and their experience becomes one of the saddest chapters in the life of Augustine. But that is getting ahead of our story.

Patricius died in 372 after converting to the faith of his wife. Meanwhile their son discovered he had a knack for public speaking, for rhetoric. It was the preferred school subject of that day, indispensable to anyone hoping for a profitable career. The art of public persuasion was absolutely required for a man who wished to get ahead in life. As an instructor in rhetoric, Augustine could earn a good living while moving up the social ladder. By the age of eighteen he was teaching rhetoric in his hometown. He also was studying the beliefs of the Manicheans. The followers of Mani (d. 276) held that the world is a contest between flesh and spirit, evil and good, darkness and light. Their philosophy combined elements from several religions of the day. Augustine was attracted to it and embraced the dualism that it posed.

Thagaste was a small town, and Augustine soon returned to Carthage where he taught rhetoric for another seven years. The pay was not what he hoped for – and neither were the students. He also continued to differ with his mother, who wept and prayed over him constantly. When at last he decided to leave Africa and try his fortune in Rome, he secretly slipped away in order to avoid her. But she quickly followed on another ship and with persistence found him in the empire's capital. The talk there was that the greatest rhetorician in Italy was not a professor, but a priest. Ambrose of Milan had a nationwide reputation for pulpit oratory, and Augustine decided to find out for himself. After a year in Rome, now at age thirty, he gathered up his mother, wife, and son and moved north to Milan. There he could teach rhetoric, at the same time learning from the technique of the great Ambrose.

By now Augustine had given up on the Manichaean system and had begun to read "Platonic books." Centuries old, the teaching of Socrates's prize pupil had gone through many later developments. The North African found it more satisfying than anything he had yet studied. At the same time he began to attend the church services where Ambrose presided and preached. He too found the priest to be brilliant, skilled, and persuasive, not only in technique but also in interpreting the Bible. Until now Augustine had despised the Jewish scriptures and their appendix called the New Testament. Compared with his Platonic books they seemed to him unsophisticated, primitive, and crude. But all that changed in the hands of Ambrose. He saw in Moses and the prophets a spiritual wisdom which culminated in Jesus Christ.

Augustine began to consider seriously the life he was living in light of what Ambrose preached. He had much to rethink because of his studies in Manichaean and Platonic thought. As weeks passed into months he gradually laid aside former ideas that did not square with Christian scripture, and he embraced what he now found in the Bible.

One hurdle stood in the way of his conversion, however – his sexual activity. He believed God was calling him to a life he could not embrace, a life of celibacy. But living without sexual pleasure seemed impossible to him. In July 386 he reached the crisis. Wrestling with his lifestyle in a time of emotional prayer, he closed his eyes and opened at random a volume of Paul's letters. The first words he saw were these: "Not in reveling and drunkenness, not in debauchery and licentiousness, not in quarreling and jealousy. Instead, put on the Lord Jesus Christ, and make no provision for the flesh, to gratify its desires" (Rom. 13:13-14 NRSV). His heart said yes, and the die was cast. From now on Augustine the passionate, eloquent African would live as a celibate Christian and teach only the scriptures.

Mother Monica was overjoyed, of course, at this answer to her prayers. Adeodatus quickly followed his father in faith, and Bishop Ambrose baptized the two in Milan on Easter Sunday 387. But what about the boy's mother, Augustine's common-law wife? Rather than marry her he followed his mother's advice. He dismissed her because she came from a social class below him. Any marriage between them would be a yoking of unequals. She returned to North Africa with neither husband nor son, and disappeared into the mists of history. Who was she? Would her family take her back? Did she too become a Christian? Did she ever marry? No one knows. From our standpoint the episode is tragic, for she and Augustine seemed to love each other deeply. But he and Monica were applying the social standards of their day, and everyone suffered for it.

Augustine continued to suffer, for within a year Monica died. She had prayed her wayward son into the Kingdom, and her mission was complete. Father and son returned home to Africa, but suffering struck again. Adeodatus died at the age of seventeen and Augustine, now thirty-five, was alone for the first time. He did have a circle of friends with whom he hoped to live in a rural setting where they could have peace to study and pray. They would be an intellectual monastic community, disciplined but loving. Within two years, however, the church in nearby Hippo Regius needed a priest, and he was pressed into service. Within another five years, now in his early forties, Augustine became their bishop. He spent the remaining thirty-three years of his life in the demanding pastoral, administrative office of bishop.

During those decades much of his energy went into answering controversial questions about the Christian faith. It was a period when the Roman Empire in Europe and North Africa was declining, a time of uncertainty and danger. Augustine wrote copiously, dictating letters and books to scribes while at the same time guiding the community of believers entrusted to his care. Three major controversies demanded his attention in the three decades of his public ministry. He wrote against the Manichaeans and their dualism, against the Donatists, a group he considered divisive, and against the Pelagians with their preference for human choice over divine grace. His correspondence was voluminous as he exchanged ideas with some of Christendom's best minds, especially the great biblical scholar Jerome.

Three books stand out as the pinnacle of Augustine's thinking and writing. In all of them he employed the rhetorical techniques he had taught, so they bear the purple tinge of passionate oratory. About ten years after his conversion he began to write his *Confessions*, the first book of its kind in the Western world. It offers a selective account of his life up to the time he was received into the church. It is a threefold confession: of sin, of faith, and of praise to God for salvation. Few books in world history have probed the human spirit so brilliantly, but today many believe from what it says that Augustine never came to understand human sexuality in a healthy way.

He wrote *On the Trinity*, the classic treatment of that doctrine in the ancient Western church. He also attempted to answer critics who were blaming obvious social decline on the followers of Jesus. He refuted that view by setting out a Christian philosophy of history in *The City of God*. He finished that giant work in 426 and died four years later on August 28, 430. At the time of his death an invading army was attacking his city, and in the next generation Rome's enemies would bring down the Empire in the West.

Augustine's call was to be a servant of God in the decline of what was, until that time, the world's greatest civilization. He knew it to be only the City of Man, however, in contrast with the true, eternal City of God. And he knew himself to be a sinner saved by grace, not a genteel soul who made a decision for Christ. In the *Confessions* he recounts a few personal episodes to illustrate the reality of sin, and he ponders the restlessness it creates in human life. "You have made us for Yourself, O God, and our hearts are restless until they find their rest in You." This famous statement clearly alludes to Jesus' invitation, "Come unto me … and I will give you rest" (Matt. 11:28). It reverberates, as we shall see, in later writers such as Bernard of Clairvaux, Julian of Norwich, Thomas à Kempis, Martin Luther, Thomas Merton – and it resonates with thoughtful Christian experience today.

In Augustine's Voice

The Confessions of St. Augustine, originally written in Latin, are available in a variety of editions and translations. The modern English version by Hal M. Helms is especially attractive for its readability. The selections reproduced here are from that translation (Brewster, MA: Paraclete Press, 1986). They retain the flavor of the orator's passionate, eloquent prose. Listen to what Augustine had to say about faith:

Praise: You are great, O Lord, and greatly to be praised. Great is your power, and your wisdom is infinite. And we would praise you; we, who are but a small particle of your creation; yes, we, though we carry with us our mortality, the evidence of our sin, the evidence that you resist the proud; yet we, but a particle of your creation, would praise you. You awake us to delight in your praise; for you made us for yourself, and our hearts are restless until they rest in you.... Oh, how shall I find rest in you? Who will send you into my heart to flood it, that I may forget my woes and embrace you, my only good? What are you to me? In your pity, teach me to speak. What am I to you, that you demand my love? ...

The House of My Soul: The house of my soul is narrow; enlarge it, that you may enter in. It is in ruins! Repair it! It has in it that which must offend your eyes. I confess and know it. But who shall cleanse it, or to whom shall I cry, but to you? Lord, cleanse me from my secret faults and spare your servant from the power of the enemy. I believe, and therefore I speak (1.1, 5, alt.).

To Steal: [At age sixteen] I had a desire to steal, and did so, compelled neither by hunger nor poverty, but through a boredom of well-doing and a lust for iniquity. For I pilfered something of which I had enough and much better. I did not care to enjoy what I stole, but rather to enjoy the act of stealing and the sin itself. There was a pear tree near our vineyard, heavily loaded with fruit that lacked both color and flavor to tempt us. To shake and rob this, some of us worthless young fellows went late one night, having prolonged our games in the streets till then, as our disgraceful habit was, and took huge loads of these pears, not to eat ourselves, but to throw to the hogs, having only tasted them, and to do this pleased us all the more because it was forbidden.

Behold my heart, O God, behold my heart, which you had pity on when it was in the bottomless pit. Let this heart of mine tell you what it sought there, that I should be evil for naught, and that my sin should have no cause but the sin itself. It was foul, and I loved it ..." (2.4).

Too late have I loved you: Too late have I loved you, O beauty, ancient yet ever new. Too late have I loved you! And behold, you were within, but I was outside, searching for you there – plunging, deformed amid those fair forms which you had made. You were with me, but I was not with you. Things held me far from you, which, unless they were in you did not exist at all. You called and shouted, and burst my deafness. You gleamed and shone upon me, and chased away my blindness. You breathed fragrant odors on me, and I held back my breath, but now I pant for you. I tasted, and now I hunger and thirst for you. You touched me, and now I yearn for your peace (10.27-28).

United: _When I come to be united with you with my whole self, I shall have no more sorrow or labor, and my life shall be wholly alive, being wholly full of you! ... but I am still a burden to myself, because I am not full of you (10.27-28).

North Africa, Augustine's home, was a large, prosperous province in the Western Roman Empire. But at the time of his death that empire was under attack on several fronts. Meanwhile, beyond France another form of Christianity was beginning to flourish, Christianity among the Celts.

3

MONASTICS AND MISSIONARIES

CELTIC CHRISTIANITY

The Roman Empire was the greatest expanse of power the ancient world ever knew. From the Straits of Gibraltar east to India, its might brought a brutal peace. All countries surrounding the Mediterranean Sea fell under its sway. But at the edges, away from the center of power, fierce tribes resisted. For example, when Julius Caesar crossed the English Channel in the first century B.C., his forces did not get far. They conquered southern England, making it part of the Roman world. But their numbers were too small and their supply lines too thin to subdue the Scots to the north. In the second century A.D. the emperor Hadrian ordered his legions to build a wall across the narrowest part of England to keep out those "barbarians." Nor did the Romans ever conquer the green island to the west – Ireland was outside the Roman Empire.

The Scots and Irish were Celts, descendants of an ancient people-group that originally stretched through much of Europe. Archaeologists have unearthed pre-Christian remains of their civilization in places such as France, Switzerland, and Turkey. France was Gaul in those days, and Paul wrote to the Galatians in Turkey – names related to Celt. But we have come to know them best through what remained of their life outside the Roman Empire, in Ireland and Scotland. For the most part they were a rural people, farmers and village-dwellers, depending on the earth for sustenance. Nature was sacred to them, and without being pantheists they saw the divine everywhere. Their leaders were clan chiefs, local kings, and druid priests, but they especially valued their poets. When Celts came together they relished storytelling, songs, and poems. As a culture, they valued women higher than in more civilized societies of that time. But they could be ferocious in warfare, when women sometimes fought alongside the men.

Christianity arrived in England early, perhaps in the first or second century. Most likely it came from France with soldiers or traders who spread the faith through the southern and western part of the island. Later, around the year 400, slave traders raided the west coast. They captured a young boy named Patrick and took him to Ireland, where a farmer bought him and set him to work herding sheep. It was a hard life, often exposed to harsh weather as well as a harsh master. During the years of his slavery Patrick prayed much and began to sense a call from God on his life. He believed God wanted him to get away, return to England, and then come back to Ireland and evangelize the Celts who had enslaved him. It was an audacious plan, and dangerous.

Details of what happened are somewhat unclear, for Patrick's story was recorded only many years later. Even the dates of his life are somewhat unsure, but the years 390-461 are often suggested, putting him a generation after Augustine. Patrick seems to have spent considerable time in England and France preparing for his mission. According to the stories told about him, he and those who accompanied him fought many spiritual battles as they brought the Irish to Christ. They had to face and defeat the druid priests, but their mission succeeded so peacefully that there were no missionary martyrs. By the time Patrick died, he was revered as a spiritual master among those who earlier had been his masters. Although not the first to evangelize Ireland, he more than anyone is identified with that country's faith. His life ended between the first plundering of Rome (451) and its final downfall in A.D. 476.

The monastic movement had traveled all the way from Egypt to Ireland, and Irish Christianity was highly monastic. It spread by starting "monastic villages" throughout the country. The monks who presided over the monasteries (sometimes both women and men) led evange-listic expansion, which placed a premium on building community. Irish Christianity assimilated some elements of the pagan past such as strong belief in God's immanence together with a love of story, song, and poetry. Prayer valued the Psalms, included the natural world, and was often lyrical. Spiritual friendship and confession were important for community, but penance could be severe. Asceticism was fierce, and its height was voluntary exile from one's home in lifelong wandering wherever the Spirit led.

Second only to Patrick in Irish veneration was Bridget (or Bride), the best-loved woman in Celtic Christianity. Sadly, what we know of her life is encrusted with layers of legend. It does seem certain that her father was a druid priest and her mother a Christian slave. Bridget assimilated much of the pagan culture into the new Christian faith. She founded a double monastery at Kildare, which she led until her death in A.D. 524.

Another leading light was the sixth-century monk Columba, a former warrior also known as Colum Cille. He was born into a noble family in County Donegal. Sailing east from Ireland, he wanted to plant the faith where he could no longer look back to his beloved home. He landed on the tiny island of Iona, off Scotland's west coast near the Isle of Mull. There, beginning in 563, Columba transformed Iona from a pagan holy site to a place sacred to Christians. He and his monks not only built a monastery; they used the island as a base for their missionary thrust into western Scotland. Iona eventually became so special that forty-eight kings of Scotland and neighboring countries were said to be buried there. Columba died in 597 and is regarded as the most illustrious Irish churchman of his time.

In the same year Gregory I, the greatest of ancient popes, ordered new Roman-style missionary work to begin in southern England. Roman Christianity, in contrast to the Celtic version, was always led by men and was hierarchical. Organization followed the top-down model of the Empire with authority emanating from the pope, the bishop of Rome. Gregory was attempting to rally the cause of Christ in the now-fallen Western Empire, and his papacy opened a new era in Europe's history.

Shortly afterward Columbanus became one of the most noted Celtic missionary monks. Starting from Ireland, this nomad wandered through France, Austria, Switzerland, and northern Italy. Wherever Columbanus went he planted monasteries and encouraged learning. By this time the desert monks of Egypt were universally known, but the Celtic monks differed from them by pursuing both learning and evangelism.

This was shown in Aidan's founding of a monastery at Lindesfarne in 635. Holy Island, as it is called, lies just off the northeast coast of England near the border with Scotland. In many respects it was to eastern England what Iona was to western Scotland – a gathered community for prayer and study, and a base for missionary outreach. Aidan was Irish-born and trained at Iona's famed monastery. In his mission to England he was loved for his gentle, understanding approach to evangelism in contrast to a Roman predecessor who had gotten nowhere. The monks on Aidan's island eventually produced the Lindesfarne Gospels. This Latin manuscript, laboriously copied and lavishly decorated, is a masterpiece from the eighth century. England's Lindesfarne Gospels and the Book of Kells (a similar manuscript from Ireland) mark the apex of Celtic art in the early Middle Ages, admired today around the world.

Other monks and monasteries followed into the middle of the seventh century. By that time Roman-style Christianity in England had worked its way northward to meet Celtic Christianity moving south out of Scotland. They agreed on substance but the question was, whose style should prevail? There were some differences. In 664 the king of Northumbria in northeast England summoned a church council at Whitby to decide the question. Hilda of Whitby was leader of a famed Celtic double monastery there, but the king ruled in favor of Roman Christianity. He reasoned that the British Isles should conform to the larger church of Western Europe.

In the years that followed, most of the Celts adopted prevailing Roman practice. Some, however, retreated to the edges of Scotland and Ireland in order to preserve their old ways. The "golden age" of Celtic Christianity extended for about another century after the council at Whitby. Shortly before the year 800, Viking raiders struck at Lindesfarne, beginning a reign of terror in England that lasted more than a century.

A later "silver age" of Celtic Christianity followed until around A.D. 1300 in the high Middle Ages. By then it was a fully Romanized church showing only traces of its early roots. Those origins came to light in the nineteenth century when patient researchers began to record the lore quietly preserved in Ireland together with the Hebrides and Orkney Islands off the coast of Scotland. This oral tradition, together with the ancient records, constitutes what today is called Celtic Christianity.

In the Celtic Voice

The best-known piece of Celtic Christian literature is the "Breastplate of Saint Patrick." Although its kernel may have originated with the saint, scholars now date the prayer to the eighth century. It comes, in other words, from the time when Celtic manuscript art was reaching its apex in the monasteries of Lindesfarne and Kells – the close of the golden age. It is a *lorica*, a breastplate, a prayer for protection. It could be prayed while dressing and lacing up the various items of clothing such as boots, tunic, belt, and cloak. The prayer is typical of Celtic Christianity in its focus on Christ, the trinity, the natural world, and the nearness of God in all things. The translation here is the work of the noted nineteenth-century author Cecil Frances Alexander. Hers is the most complete poetic version. [*A Guide to Prayer for Ministers and Other Servants*, ed. by Reuben P. Job and Norman Shawchuck. (Nashville: The Upper Room, 1983, p. 309)].

A Lorica

I bind unto myself today
The strong Name of the Trinity,
By invocation of the same,
The Three in One, and One in Three.

I bind this day to me forever,
By power of faith, Christ's Incarnation;
His baptism in the Jordan river;
His death on the cross for my salvation;
His bursting from the spiced tomb;
His riding up the heav'nly way;
His coming at the day of doom:
I bind unto myself today.

I bind unto myself the power
Of the great love of cherubim;
The sweet "Well done" in judgment hour;
The service of the seraphim:
Confessors' faith, apostles' word,
The patriarchs' prayers, the prophets' scrolls;
All good deeds done unto the Lord,
And purity of virgin souls.

I bind unto myself today
The virtues of the starlit heav'n,
The glorious sun's life-giving ray,
The whiteness of the moon at even,
The flashing of the lightning free,
The whirling wind's tempestuous shocks,
The stable earth, the deep salt sea,
Around the old eternal rocks.

I bind unto myself today
The power of God to hold and lead,
His eye to watch, his might to stay,
His ear to hearken to my need;
The wisdom of my God to teach,
His hand to guide, his shield to ward;
The word of God to give me speech,
His heav'nly host to be my guard.

Christ be with me, Christ within me,
Christ behind me, Christ before me,
Christ beside me, Christ to win me,
Christ to comfort and restore me,
Christ beneath me, Christ above me,
Christ in quiet, Christ in danger,
Christ in hearts of all that love me,
Christ in mouth of friend and stranger.

I bind unto myself the Name,
The strong Name of the Trinity;
By invocation of the same,
The Three in One, and One in Three,
Of whom all nature hath creation;
Eternal Father, Spirit, Word:
Praise to the Lord of my salvation,
Salvation is of Christ the Lord.

Amen.

Another masterpiece of Celtic Christian literature is the poem known in its hymn form as "Be Thou My Vision." Like the final version of St. Patrick's Breastplate, it is dated to the eighth century. Originally in Irish, it was translated into English prose by Mary Elizabeth Byrne in 1905. Then in 1912 Eleanor Hull versified it for singing in the form we know today. This prayer is remarkable iety of its God-images and the tender way in which it conceives of the Almighty.

A Hymn

Be thou my vision, O Lord of my heart;
Naught be all else to me save that thou art.
Thou my best thought, by day or by night,
Waking or sleeping, thy presence my light.

Be thou my wisdom, be thou my true word;
I ever with thee, and thou with me, Lord.
Thou my great Father, thy child may I be,
Thou in me dwelling, and I one with thee.

Be thou my buckler, my sword for the fight.
Be thou my dignity, thou my delight,
Thou my soul's shelter, thou my high tower.
Raise thou me heav'nward, O Pow'r of my pow'r.

Riches I heed not, nor vain empty praise;
Thou mine inheritance, now and always.
Thou and thou only, first in my heart,
High King of heaven, my treasure thou art.

High King of heaven, when vict'ry is won
May I reach heaven's joys, O bright heav'n's Sun!
Heart of my own heart, whatever befall,
Still be my vision, O Ruler of all.

Columba (A.D. 521-597) of Iona is one of the most famous Celtic saints. Here is a beautiful prayer said to come from his pen.

A Prayer

Almighty Father, Son and Holy Ghost, eternal ever blessed gracious God; to me, the least of saints, to me allow that I may keep a door in paradise. That I may keep even the smallest door, the furthest, the darkest, coldest door, the door that is least used, the stiffest door. If so it be but in thine house, O God, if so be that I can see thy glory even afar, and hear thy voice O God, and know that I am with thee, thee O God [Columba, *The Oxford Book of Prayer*, ed. by George Appleton (New York: Oxford University Press, 1985), p. 145].

Much has been written in recent years about Celtic spirituality, not all of it well informed or wise. Among the more reliable guides are Esther DeWaal's tiny introduction *God Under My Roof* (Paraclete Press, 1984) and her later, more extensive treatment, *The Celtic Way of Prayer* (Doubleday, 1997). *Celtic Christianity* by Timothy Joyce, O.S.B. (Orbis Press, 1998), is a brief, reliable historical survey. Oliver Davies and Fiona Bowie have produced one of the best anthologies in *Celtic Christian Spirituality* (Continuum, 1995). Davies also edited *Celtic Spirituality* in the series Classics of Western Spirituality (Paulist Press, 1999). Alexander Carmichael's *Carmina Gadelica*, the classic collection of traditional oral material published a century ago, has been reprinted in a one-volume edition (Edinburgh: Floris Books, 1992).

We now leave the Celts for France, encountering Bernard of Clairvaux. A very gifted man, he wrote prose and poetry, was a student of theology, and a prolific correspondent.

4

MELLIFLUOUS DOCTOR

BERNARD OF CLAIRVAUX

It is well known that John Calvin was a theological son of the great Augustine of Hippo. Calvin's next-favorite author (aside from scripture) was the saintly Bernard of Clairvaux. This French Catholic monk wrote in such a way that the French-speaking Protestant could easily cite him in his writings. But four centuries separated them — four significant centuries.

Bernard was born in 1090 or 1091 in Burgundy, France's famed wine country. Although his parents were of the nobility, his mother believed in living on less rather than more. Thus Bernard grew up in austere circumstances, worshiping God and attending school. He proved to be a gifted pupil with superior intellect and charming personality. But one gospel text kept calling him to something more: "Come to me, all you who labor and are heavy ladened, and I will give you rest" (Matt. 11:28 NKJV).

Bernard knew that he (like Augustine before him) wanted rest for his soul, and he wished to take up the yoke of Christ (Matt. 11:29). Thus at age twenty-one he became a monk at Citeaux. His example and persuasion were so attractive that he brought with him thirty other young nobles, including his own brothers. Within four years still more had joined them and, at the pope's direction, they founded a new monastery in Champagne at Clairvaux. Under Bernard's leadership this daughter house of Citeaux rapidly became a center of the Cistercian

Order – Benedictines of the Strict Observance (abbreviated O.C.S.O.). The Benedictine Order, now five hundred years old, was the premier monastic order in Europe. With its motto of "prayer and work," most other groups took their cue from it, leaning to the left or right. But it needed renewal, which is what the Cistercians were about. They wanted a return to the original ideals with strict observance of prayer, manual labor, silence, and seclusion from the world. Bernard's strong personality, great intelligence, and deep spirituality quickly established him as the Order's dominant figure.

Under his leadership the Cistercians experienced explosive growth, increasing in his lifetime to 350 monasteries, almost half of them under his authority. In that role he traveled extensively throughout Western Europe on missions for the pope, which gave him great influence in the operations of the church. He denounced persecution of the Jews and insisted that all Christians – lay and religious – should live lives of prayer, worship, and self-denial. When a dispute arose in 1130 over who was the rightful pope, Bernard's candidate prevailed, and the grateful winner showered privileges on the Cistercian Order. Fifteen years later Bernard gained even more power when one of his former pupils became the newest pope.

Now by some accounts the most influential man in Europe, Bernard entered many levels of controversy, both theological and ecclesiastical. He became especially noted as the pope's spokesman for promoting the Second Crusade (1147). The First Crusade (1095-1100) had succeeded in capturing Antioch and Jerusalem for the Christians. The Second Crusade intended to relieve the pressure Muslim forces were putting on European armies and their settlements in the East. Bernard traveled widely to raise money and recruit men for the cause but, much to his disappointment and disgrace, it failed.

Bernard wrote voluminously in his role as promoter of the Cistercian Order. According to some accounts his total output in Latin amounts to about thirty-five hundred pages. He is said to have composed one thousand letters, of which 469 survive, some of them correspondence with the great Hildegard of Bingen in the Rhineland. Like her, Bernard was a songwriter and poet, theologian and mystic. He composed treatises on humility, pride, grace, free choice, and above all, love. In theological discussions about predestination, he was famous for saying, "Remove free-will and there is nothing to be saved; remove grace and there is left no means of saving. The work of salvation cannot be accomplished without the cooperation of the two." The Bible was prominent in his writings, the book of Canticles (Song of Songs or Song of Solomon) being a special favorite. He delivered eighty-six sermons to his monks from just its opening verses! The humanity of Jesus was coming into prominence in his day, and that was true for Bernard as well. Well-known hymns such as "O Sacred Head Now Wounded" and "Jesus, the Very Thought of Thee" have been attributed to him, but he is no longer thought to be their author.

Bernard died in 1153 at the age of sixty-three, and just twenty-one years later the Catholic Church canonized him as Saint Bernard. His brilliant writings influenced many who came after him, including such Protestants as Martin Luther and John Calvin. In 1830 he was proclaimed a Doctor or universal teacher of the Church, an honor bestowed on only a handful of persons. Pope Pius XII in 1953 described him as the "Mellifluous Doctor" or sweet-sounding teacher because of the style and substance of his writings.

Bernard of Clairvaux is still widely read today as a guide in spiritual formation. His book *On the Love of God* is especially noted for its insight into the Christian journey. At first, he says, we experience infantile love, love of self for self's sake. Some have called this carnal or fleshly love, love easily enslaved to self-centered physical desires. We want God for personal satisfaction and instant gratification. But if we truly seek God's rule in all things we will bear restraint rather than allow sin to reign in our bodily life. And we will progress to the second stage, which is mercenary love, love of God for self's sake. We treat the Holy One as a heavenly vending machine who dispenses favors for the appropriate price or prayer. Realizing that we can do nothing without God, we use the divine for our human ends. We are mercenary, loving God for what we can get.

With much practice we may proceed to a more mature experience, love of God for God's sake. Now we ask for little, but allow God's love to motivate us rather than be motivated by our own needs or wants. We become more passionate about the Giver than the gifts. Some have likened this to a mature child's love for a good parent, and it is as far as many believers ever go. But, says Bernard, there is yet one more stage, a fourth: loving ourselves for God's sake. We can come by grace to respect, care for, and value ourselves as God values us. Some have likened this to marriage between two persons who profoundly trust, regard, and love each other. For Bernard, this will never be our attainment, but always God's gift. And he believed the experience is rare, even momentary, because in our present existence it is so hard to maintain perfect love.

Dr. Wayne Oates, a pioneer in the field of pastoral counseling, compared Bernard's four loves with what we know from developmental psychology. He referred to them as the survival love of an infant, the prudential love of a small child, a youth's unselfish love, and the unconditional love of an adult. Bernard's exposition of love, like that by Julian of Norwich, resonates with 1 John 4:7-21, a scripture passage worth studying in detail and pondering at length.

In Bernard's Voice

Bernard's book *On the Love of God* was briefly outlined above. Here are selected excerpts to give a taste of his writing.

Love of Self: In the human realm people love themselves for their own sake. But if this love of ourselves becomes too lavish, it will overflow its natural boundaries through excessive love of pleasure. People can easily become slaves to the soul's enemy: lust. But what will you do if your own needs are not met? Will you look to God to meet your needs? Seeking first the kingdom means to prefer to bear the yoke of modesty and restraint rather than allow sin to reign in your mortal body.

All Things Through Him: When we suffer some calamity, some storm in our lives, we turn to God and ask his help, calling upon him in times of trouble. This is how we who only love ourselves first begin to love God. We will begin to love God even if it is for our own sake. We love God because we have learned that we can do all things through him, and without him we can do nothing.

The Grace of the Rescuer: But if trials and tribulations continue to come upon us, every time God brings us through, even if our hearts were made of stone, we will begin to be softened because of the grace of the Rescuer. Thus, we begin to love God not merely for our own sakes, but for himself. Thus it happens that once God's sweetness has been tasted, it draws us to the pure love of God more than our needs compel us to love him. We have obtained this degree when we can say, "Give praise to the Lord for he is good, not because he is good to me, but because he is good." Thus we truly love God for God's sake and not for our own.

The Fourth Degree of Love: Blessed are we who experience the fourth degree of love wherein we love ourselves for God's sake. Such experiences are rare and come only for a moment. Just as a drop of water mixed with a lot of wine seems to entirely lose its own identity as it takes on the taste and color of the wine, just as iron, heated and glowing, looks very much like fire, having lost its original appearance, just as air flooded with the light of the sun is transformed into the same splendor of the light so that it appears to be light itself, so it is like for those who melt away from themselves and are entirely transfused into the will of God.

I am not certain that the fourth degree of love in which we love ourselves only for the sake of God may be perfectly attained in this life. But, when it does happen, we will experience the joy of the Lord and be forgetful of ourselves in a wonderful way. We are, for those moments, one mind and one spirit with God" [condensed from *Devotional*

Classics: Selected Readings for Individuals and Groups, ed. by Richard J. Foster and James Bryan Smith. HarperSanFrancisco, 1993, pp. 40-43].

Born about thirty years after Bernard's death, of Italian descent, Francis of Assisi has less of an established biography, some of which resembles legend more than fact. His pattern of poverty and simplicity is well-remembered, and while perhaps not as prolific as Bernard, his influence stretches around the globe today.

5

THE LITTLE POOR MAN

FRANCIS OF ASSISI

An Italian baby was born in 1181 or 1182 while his father was away in France on business. His mother named her newborn son Giovanni (John). But when her husband returned, he renamed the baby Francesco because he was so impressed with France — and that is how Francis of Assisi got his name. The story of his life is somewhat uncertain because the quest for the historical Francis is nearly as complex as the quest for the historical Jesus. Written accounts about him come from a generation or more after his death, many of them in a collection called the *Fioretti* (little flowers or bouquet), which seems to be a mixture of fact, legend, and piety. What scholars have been able to agree on goes something like this.

Francis had a normal early life in Assisi where he attended the parish school. As a teenager he was a merrymaker who enjoyed parties, hanging out with his buddies, and singing loudly in the streets at night. Italy at this time was a collage of city-states often at war with one another. By the time Francis was twenty he had fought in an inter-city battle where he was captured. His father, a well-to-do cloth merchant, paid a ransom for his son's freedom, but afterward Francis endured a long illness.

The next year he was feeling well enough to set out on one of the Crusades, but a vision directed him to return home to seek God's will. Francis's gradual conversion had begun. He started to give generously to the poor and did the unthinkable when he publicly embraced a leper. Townspeople, believing him to be mentally unbalanced, began to mock him, but Francis sought solitude in nearby caves and abandoned churches. One day in 1205, while praying in the little run-down church of San Damiano (St. Damien), he thought Jesus spoke to him from the crucifix: "Go, repair my house which, as you see, is falling completely to ruin." In order to refurbish the chapel Francis helped himself to expensive cloth from his father's import shop, sold it, and used the money to repair the building. His unsympathetic father was so angry that he brought his son before the bishop of Assisi, demanding repayment for the stolen cloth. In response Francis stripped off his own clothing, renounced his inheritance, and declared that henceforth only God would be his father.

Francis continued his work of begging stones to repair dilapidated churches and also nursed lepers in their illness. Desiring to imitate Jesus more completely, he began to preach evangelistically, traveling around the countryside with no financial support. Poverty and simplicity were his watchwords following the gospel injunction, "Take no gold, or silver, or copper in your belts, no bag for your journey, or two tunics, or sandals, or a staff; for laborers deserve their food" (Matt. 10:9-10 NRSV). He was so intent on this that he became known as *il poverello*, the little poor man. When asked about marriage, he said he was already married – to Lady Poverty.

His example so inspired other young men that several left their families and fortunes to join Francis. As their numbers increased he wrote a Rule, a constitution for their new Order. They would not be monastics but mendicants, wandering preachers who earned their living by begging. Honoring humility, they called themselves "little brothers," the Order of Friars Minor (O.F.M.). Francis traveled to Rome in 1209 to gain the pope's approval for the Order, then returned to Assisi. There the group settled at the small chapel of St. Mary of the Angels, the Portiuncula or "little portion."

Their evangelistic preaching and humble living attracted many people, for the church was rife with bureaucracy, wealth, and graft. The numbers increased, and women of faith wanted to come alongside the men. So in 1212 Francis formally received Chiara (Clare) di Favarone, an eighteen-year-old friend, as the founding member of the Second Order. These women were not free to travel like the men but gave themselves to prayer, living quiet lives in cloistered houses. Their highly disciplined Order is known today as the Poor Clares. Francis and Clare remained close friends throughout the remainder of their lives, although they seldom saw each other and then only under restricted circumstances.

The year 1213 proved to be important for Francis. He received the gift of a mountain named La Verna, where he often went for solitude. That year also marked the first general assembly of the Order, which quickly grew to five thousand brothers by 1217. Francis was now seeking volunteers to evangelize in Germany, Tunis, and Syria, and eventually in Spain and England. He himself traveled to the Holy Land and then to Egypt, where he tried to persuade the Muslim sultan to follow Christ. His sincerity and courage impressed the sultan who listened attentively, then sent him on his way. In contrast, the immorality and cruelty of the Christian armies from Europe filled the gentle friar with disgust. His reputation for kindness extended even to animals.

The Order grew so rapidly that the pope told Francis he had to establish more discipline among the brothers. Knowing his own poor administrative skills, Francis appointed one of the men to lead as minister general and instituted the novitiate, a probationary period for new members. After much debate Francis also wrote a new Rule for the Order, which the pope approved in 1223. At Christmas in the town of Greccio he popularized the nativity story by using live animals to reenact the account of Jesus' birth, virtually creating the modern crèche.

But "the little poor man," now in his early forties, was exhausted and ill. Poverty and fasting, preaching and travel had taken their toll on his body. His ministry had become such a whirlwind that in 1224 he returned to his beloved La Verna for a period of retreat. His life of prayer was well known, and one of the brothers had been converted years earlier by observing how Francis prayed through the night. All the brother heard him say was, "My God and my all! My God and my all!" – pure adoration, with petition perhaps implied. Now back at La Verna, Francis was giving himself to prayer. During a September all-night prayer vigil he developed bloody marks or stigmata in his hands, feet, and side, marks that looked like nail-prints and a spear wound. No earlier reports of such experience existed, and Francis was baffled by what had happened in his body. The wounds did not heal, so he tried to hide them with clothing, but a few brothers close to him learned of their existence. He felt intense pain if anyone touched them, and the brothers worked to be gentle as they helped their suffering leader with his clothing.

By the spring of 1225 Francis was nearly blind, but he managed to travel back to San Damiano, where Jesus had spoken to him twenty years before. There his friend Clare and the sisters with her cared for him as best they could. Despite his agonies, he managed to compose most of "The Canticle of the Sun," a poem celebrating God's goodness in creation and its beauty. It speaks of Brother Sun and Sister Moon, Brother Fire and Sister Water together with herbs, flowers, and fruit, everything that makes human life pleasant and joyful. In an attempt to halt his increasing blindness doctors persuaded him to let them cauterize his temples, but the hideous procedure did no good and he only grew weaker.

In September 1226 Francis asked to be taken back to the Portiuncula where he and the original brothers had lived together. There he composed some final lines for the "Canticle," especially about Sister Death, who came for him on October 3. Within only two years he was canonized as Saint Francis. The Catholic Church was so impressed with the life and ministry of *il poverello* that they built an enormous church in Assisi to honor him. There his earthly remains rest today in the Basilica of St. Francis. He is possibly the most beloved of all Catholic saints, now the patron of ecology, and definitely a classic friend. Franciscans in all their branches are the largest Order in the world.

In Francis' Voice

Francis is remembered not so much for what he wrote as for what he did and who he was. His simple humility, gentle kindness, and extreme poverty have become proverbial. But he and Clare did write several kinds of material that have come down to us. Again, determining authenticity is difficult, but several of Clare's letters to Agnes of Prague remain. Blessed Agnes, as she is known, was of royal birth and desired by famous men as a wife, but she avoided marriage and lived fifty-four years as a Poor Clare. Various writings of Francis also have been declared genuine, but the familiar "The Prayer of St. Francis" which begins "Lord, make me an instrument of thy peace" is not among them. Although its spirit seems authentic, its existence prior to the nineteenth century has not been verified.

The best source for study will likely be *Francis and Clare: The Complete Works*, a volume in The Classics of Western Spirituality (New York: Paulist Press, 1982). The *Little Flowers of Saint Francis*, translated by Raphael Brown, is a standard translation of the *Fioretti*, the ancient stories, some fact, some legend, that gathered around the saint (New York: Doubleday, 1958). A mountain of popular material about Francis has also been published. One helpful work of this kind is by monk and musician John Michael Talbot with Steve Rabey, *The Lessons of St. Francis: How to Bring Simplicity and Spirituality into Your Daily Life* (New York: Penguin, 1997). Talbot has also produced several recordings of original music using texts by St. Francis.

Of his genuine writings, "The Canticle of the Sun" is undoubtedly the most famous. Its paean to the creator of all existence and beauty is unsurpassed. Like Psalm 148, it speaks first of the heavenly bodies, then turns to air, water, fire, and Sister Earth, our mother. Shortly before his death Francis convinced two warring cities to be reconciled, which he may refer to as "those who grant pardon for love of You." Then, before mentioning Sister Death, he mentions "those who endure sickness and trial ... in peace," perhaps referring to his own experience as well as that of others. The final lines are typical of Francis,

43

calling on everyone to praise, bless, and thank "my Lord," and "serve him with great humility." Many churches include a versified form of the Canticle in their hymnals as "All Creatures of Our God and King."

The Canticle of Brother Sun

Most high, all-powerful, all good, Lord!
All praise is yours, all glory, all honor
And all blessing.
To you, alone, Most High, do they belong.
No mortal lips are worthy
To pronounce your name.
All praise be yours, my Lord, through all that you have made,
And first my lord Brother Sun,
Who brings the day; and light you give to us through him.
How beautiful is he, how radiant in all his splendor!
Of you, Most High, he bears the likeness.

All praise be yours, my Lord, through Sister Moon and Stars;
In the heavens you have made them, bright
And precious and fair.

All praise be yours, my Lord, through Brothers Wind and Air,
And fair and stormy, all the weather's moods,
By which you cherish all that you have made.

All praise be yours, my Lord, through Sister Water,
So useful, lowly, precious and pure.

All praise be yours, my Lord, through Brother Fire,
Through whom you brighten up the night.
How beautiful is he, how gay! Full of power and strength.

All praise be yours, my Lord, through Sister Earth, our mother,
Who feeds us in her sovereignty and produces
Various fruits with colored flowers and herbs.
All praise be yours, my Lord, through those who grant pardon
For love of you; through those who endure
Sickness and trial.
Happy those who endure in peace,
By you, Most High, they will be crowned.

All praise be yours, my Lord, through Sister Death,
From whose embrace no mortal can escape.
Woe to those who die in mortal sin!
Happy those she finds doing your will!
The second death can do no harm to them.
Praise and bless my Lord, and give him thanks,
And serve him with great humility.

[*St. Francis of Assisi: Omnibus of Sources*, ed. by M. A. Habig. 2nd ed. (London: SPCK, 1979), p. 130f. Cited in *The Lord of the Journey: A Reader in Christian Spirituality*, ed. by Roger Pooley and Philip Seddon. (London: Collins Liturgical Publications, 1986), p. 52ff.]

A second authentic writing is "The Parchment Given to Brother Leo." Friends guarded the original copy signed by Francis in 1224, and it is preserved today at Assisi in the Basilica of St. Francis. Side one, "the praises of God," catalogues attributes and virtues of the one he calls Lord, only God, the most high, almighty King, Holy Father, King of heaven and earth, Three and One, Lord God of gods. Then follows a list of mercies toward humanity, all addressed directly to the Holy One. "You are love," it begins, and concludes with "You are our eternal life: Great and wonderful Lord, God almighty, Merciful Savior." Side two of the parchment contains the priestly Aaronic blessing from the Hebrew scriptures (Num. 6:24-26), here addressed to Brother Leo, who noted that Francis wrote it less than two years before his death.

The Praises of God

THE MANUSCRIPT GIVEN TO BROTHER LEO
You are holy, Lord, the only God. You do wonders.
You are strong, you are great, you are the most high,
You are the almighty King.
You, Holy Father, the King of heaven of earth.
You are good, all good, the highest good,
Lord, God, living and true.

You are love, charity.
You are wisdom; you are humility; you are patience;
you are beauty; you are meekness; you are security;
you are inner peace; you are joy; you are our hope and joy;
you are justice; you are moderation, you are all our riches
you are enough for us.

You are beauty, you are meekness;
you are the protector,
you are our guardian and defender;
you are strength; you are refreshment.

You are our hope, you are our faith, you are our charity,
you are all our sweetness,
you are our eternal life:
great and wonderful Lord,
God almighty, Merciful Saviour.

[*Francis and Clare: The Complete Works,* ed. by R. J. Armstrong and I. C. Brady. Classics of Western Spirituality. (London: SPCK, 1982), p. 99f. Cited in *The Lord of the Journey: A Reader in Christian Spirituality,* ed. by Roger Pooley and Philip Seddon (London: Collins Liturgical Publications, 1986), p. 36f.]

While Francis's call was to be an itinerant evangelist, others at this time were called to a different kind of service. Among them was Julian of Norwich whose life was different indeed – very different.

6

SERIOUS OPTIMIST

JULIAN OF NORWICH

People who enjoy a good mystery may also like Julian of Norwich. This woman of prayer lived for decades in a tiny apartment or cell attached to the church of St. Julian in Norwich, England. She is called by the name of that church, but who she was or how she got there or what became of her, no one knows. At her death she left behind the first book written in English by a woman. Thomas Merton, whose learning was encyclopedic, valued her as one of the two greatest English theologians, far better, he said, than all the Spanish mystics taken together. We know her today as both a uniquely creative theologian and a devotional writer of extraordinary optimism and grace.

Julian was born in 1342 and lived through one of the most horrific periods in England's history. When she was seven years old the bubonic plague, after sweeping through Europe, jumped the English Channel and killed one-third of her country's population. No one understood its cause or cure. Conventional wisdom held it to be the judgment of God's anger upon the kingdom. It returned a dozen years later, this time especially striking down young children. Its terror appeared in Norwich for the third time in 1368, when Julian was twenty-six. The disease – variously called the black death for the way it darkened the skin or bubonic plague for its trademark buboes (swellings) – killed its victims in a matter of days, sometimes within hours.

As if this were not enough, the fourteenth century in general was one of the hardest in England's history. The era was marked by prolonged war because the king of England was claiming to be also the king of France. Internal unrest took violent form in 1381 in a peasants' revolt against the monarchy. At the same time Oxford University professor John Wycliffe began translating the New Testament from Greek into English. The university, considered the spiritual center of England, expelled him when he attacked the papacy as Antichrist. In the years that followed some who adopted his ideas were burned at the stake less than two miles from the church of St. Julian.

No one knows just when the woman we call Julian came to live at the church, but her action was not unusual for that time. She was an anchoress, a professional intercessor and spiritual director in residence. The vocation was popular enough that manuals were developed for its conduct and practice. If Julian's situation followed the manuals, she would have lived in one or two small rooms attached to the church. Possibly a walled garden area would be just outside. Her tiny apartment or cell would have a window, the squint, into the church through which she could observe the daily hours of prayer and receive the bread of the eucharist, as only priests received the wine. Another window would look into the street, in her case the busy road southwest toward London. If she was available for conversation, the window would be open but covered with a white cloth to hide her face. And we know that Julian was available, for Margery Kempe, famed for her travel to holy sites, recorded that she visited Julian, who encouraged her with her good advice.

The manuals for anchoresses allowed them to have a servant who could bring in provisions and run necessary errands. They also could have a cat for companionship and rodent control. Their task was to pray – pray with the church in its hours of worship and pray for the church in every conceivable way. Everything was grist for prayer: births, baptisms, confirmations, marriages, deaths, planting, harvesting, herds, flocks, king and country, bishop and priest, city and parish.

Anything could be subject for prayer together with the cultivation of one's own soul.

No one knows how long Julian lived this kind of life or when she died. In her later years she received money from several bequests, the last in 1416 when she would have been in her mid-seventies. She died sometime after that, but when or where she was laid to rest remains a mystery. By the time her life ended, the Italian Renaissance was in full bloom, Robin Hood had appeared in popular English literature, Geoffrey Chaucer had written his *Canterbury Tales*, Joan of Arc was born (1412), and Professor Jan Hus had been burned alive for promoting Wycliffe's ideas at the University of Prague (1415). Within a century a German professor named Luther would light the fires of the Reformation, changing forever the history and character of Europe.

An early scribe who copied Julian's book called it *Revelations of Divine Love*, but Julian preferred to call her experiences simply *Showings*. She expounds a series of visions and words from the Lord which she received at the age of thirty in May 1373. Julian had prayed to identify so closely with Christ's sufferings that she could feel what he felt. She became gravely ill, and a parish priest administered the church's last rites. When he left Julian, he placed a crucifix before her and encouraged her to take comfort from the one who suffered on the cross for her. As she tried to focus on the crucifix Christ seemed to speak to her. Sixteen "showings" followed in the next twenty-four hours, after which they stopped and she fully recovered. What Julian experienced during that time and how she understood it is what her book contains.

The basic message is that God's love for us is so all-encompassing it meets every need and satisfies every longing. She concludes that in all God showed her and told her, "love was his meaning." If that is true, then "all shall be well, and all shall be well, and all manner of thing shall be well." These statements, perhaps her most memorable ones, come at the end of the book, which describes her sixteen "showings" in eighty-six chapters.

She begins by relating her dying experience and the vision she had of the dying Christ. Her vision of his body hanging in a dry, icy wind is especially striking. But more important to Julian is that Jesus did this out of love for her and all believers – and if he could do more, he would. True love produces both sacrifice and joy, and he speaks to her of both. Although a handful of early chapters contain graphic descriptions of his suffering (especially chapters 10, 12, 16-21), Julian writes mostly about the love of God in Christ, from which nothing can separate us.

One of the book's most famous passages is the hazelnut vision of chapter 5 which contains echoes of Augustine's *Confessions*. It speaks of our restlessness apart from the God who made us for himself. The mystery of Julian deepens because no one knows whether she had read Augustine (assuming she could read) or merely heard his kind of language where she was. Of course, behind both the African orator and the English visionary lie the words of Jesus: "Come to me, all you that are weary and are carrying heavy burdens, and I will give you rest. Take my yoke upon you, and learn from me; for I am gentle and humble in heart, and you will find rest for your souls" (Matt. 11:28-29 NKJV).

Julian loves to employ threefold statements in her writing. Even more, she is thoroughly trinitarian in her thinking and Christocentric in focus. As she says, "Where Jesus appears the blessed Trinity is understood" (chapter 4). She takes three chief attributes of God and identifies them with the members of the Trinity: the power or might of the Father, the wisdom of the Son, and the Spirit's goodness or love. She would have enjoyed the 1988 praise song by Rich Mullins that sang of the awesomeness of God, his heavenly reign, and the wisdom, power and love that is his being. For Julian, God as Father, Son, and Holy Spirit is all mighty, all wise, and all good.

Present-day writers call Jesus Lord, as Julian does, but she also refers to the Holy Spirit as Lord. In doing so she echoes the ancient Nicene and Athanasian creeds which speak of "the Lord the Spirit." Following biblical precedent, she flexes between God as God and the Father as God. But when it comes to the Son, Julian explodes in creativity. She employs a whole volley of terms for who Christ Jesus is to us: brother, savior, spouse, friend, lord – he is, in fact, our heaven (chapter 19).

Julian has received much attention in our day because she also calls Jesus our mother. She sees in him the tenderness and nurturing which people often identify with motherhood. But there is more. Julian also sees in Jesus the wisdom of God – compassionate, profound, truthful understanding. When the Bible was read in her church, always in Latin, the term "wisdom" was feminine. In ancient Hebrew and Greek, as well as Latin, wisdom is a feminine term. Many people associate wisdom with a grandmother or another woman rich in experience – a spiritual mother. For Julian, Jesus is the mother whose pain on the cross gave birth to the church and who continues to nourish his people through word and sacrament. But Julian does not replace God the Father with God the Mother. Instead, she cracks the rules of grammar when she writes, "Jesus our mother, he does …," or "he says …."

However motherly Jesus is, for Julian he is always Lord. She sees him as a joyful monarch, ranging through a great banquet hall to greet his guests and make them at home in his home (chapter 14). Jesus is, in fact, both "courteous" and "homely." He has all the dignity and manners of the royal court; at the same time he enjoys being at home with the least of his subjects. No one is too small or unnoticed for his attention, and that care is all wise, all mighty, and all loving. Our experience may alternate between weal and woe; our lives can swing like pendulums between despair and joy. But Jesus' desire is always for our comfort in both solace and strength. From time to time Julian notes that what she saw and heard is for all Christians, for Christ wants us to rest in him, love him, and enjoy him forever.

Sin and its effects are what bother us, and Julian too. If God is love, as Julian says, why then do we suffer? Even more, why does God allow sin in the world? Julian received no answer to this in her revelations. It remained for her, as for us, the great unresolved tension of life. What she did hear was a word from God: at the last day there will be "a great deed" in which God will make all things right, and so all shall be well. Only God knows the details of that deed or its date, and we are not to speculate about it. "For I saw truly in our Lord's intention that the more we busy ourselves in that or in anything else, the further we shall be from knowing" (chapter 33). Instead, we are to remember what God has already done, learn from that, and so rest in him. We are to persevere in believing, trusting, and risking all in love.

With that sunny faith, that serious optimism, Julian asserts what she learned in her showings: "All shall be well, and all shall be well, and all manner of thing shall be well," her famous statement first mentioned in chapter 27. This is no mindless self-hypnosis. It grows, rather, out of her immersion in scripture. She would have heard the Psalms in her church every day through all her years as an anchoress. Her writing gives evidence of being especially formed by the Fourth Gospel and the letters of Paul. Her general tone echoes the triumphant conclusion of Romans 8 that nothing can separate us from the love of God which is in Christ Jesus our Lord. Her *Showings* seem almost to be an extended meditation on ideas and language such as that truth, and this: "God is love, and those who abide in love abide in God, and God abides in them.... There is no fear in love, but perfect love casts out fear; for fear has to do with punishment, and whoever fears has not reached perfection in love. We love because he first loved us" (1 John 4:16b, 18-19 NRSV).

In Julian's Voice

For a small sample of Julian's teaching, try *Encounter with God's Love: Selected Writings of Julian of Norwich*, edited by Keith Beasley-Topliffe (Nashville: Upper Room Books, 1998). Here, in just sixty-six pages, is an excellent introduction and a selection of material, all in the best of present-day language.

For the tiniest taste, try *Daily Readings with Julian of Norwich, volume 1*, edited by Robert Llewelyn (Springfield, IL: Templegate Publishers, 1980). These excerpted quotations are arranged under subject headings for daily use over a period of two months. This is a beautiful little book for pocket or purse, perusal and pondering.

Chapter 5 of Julian's *Showings* contains her hazelnut vision, possibly the most famous passage in the book. God shows her the entire universe as small as a hazelnut in the palm of a hand. As she writes, she echoes Augustine's sentiment about our restlessness apart from God. Her voice echoes through the centuries as we listen to her vision.

A Hazelnut: At this time our Lord showed me an inward sight of his homely loving. I saw that he is everything that is good and comforting to us. He is our clothing. In his love he wraps and holds us. He enfolds us in love and he will never let us go.

And then he showed me a little thing, the size of a hazelnut, in the palm of my hand – and it was as round as a ball. I looked at it with my mind's eye and I thought: 'What can this be?' And answer came: 'It is all that is made.' I marveled that it could last, for I thought it might have crumbled to nothing, it was so small. And the answer came into my mind: 'It lasts, and ever shall, because God loves it.' ...

In this little thing I saw three truths. The first is that God made it. The second is that God loves it. And the third is that God looks after it.

We need to know how small creation is ... if we are to love and have God who is not created. For this is the reason we are not at rest in heart and soul – that here we seek rest in things that are so little there is no rest in them – and we do not know our God who is all-mighty, all-wise, and all-good. For he is true rest. God's will is that we know him, and it rejoices him when we rest in him. For all that is less than him cannot satisfy us.

God's Goodness: God, of your goodness, give me yourself, for you are enough for me. There is nothing less I can ask that is worthy of you, and if I ask for anything less I shall be always lacking, for only in you I have all.'

For his goodness encompasses all his creatures, and all his blessed works. He has made us for himself alone, and has restored us by his blessed Passion, and keeps us in his blessed love. And he does all this through his goodness [*All Shall Be Well: Daily Readings from Julian of Norwich,* abridged and arranged by Sheila Upjohn. (Harrisburg, PA: Morehouse Publishing, 1992), p. 4, from chapter 5].

Julian concludes her twenty years of meditation in *Showings* with a ringing affirmation of the love of God, and the God of love.

An Affirmation: What, do you wish to know your Lord's meaning in this thing? Know it well, love was his meaning. Who reveals it to you? Love. What did he reveal to you? Love. Why does he reveal it to you? For love. Remain in this, and you will know more of the same. But you will never know different, without end. So I was taught that love is our Lord's meaning. And I saw very certainly in this and in everything that before God made us he loved us, which love was never abated and never will be.... In our creation we had beginning, but the love in which he created us was in him from without beginning. In this love we have our beginning, and all this shall we see in God without end (chapter 86).

Because *Showings* is a rather large book, and sometimes repetitious, you may want to select a few of its most outstanding passages such as these:

Chapters 1-11: Julian and Jesus in their dying
Chapters 22-24: Jesus' joyful love for us
Chapters 32-33: "The great deed" of the future
Chapters 41-43: Prayer as asking, thanking, and resting
Chapter 52: Our mixed human experience (weal and woe)
Chapters 58-59: A synthesis of her teaching on the Trinity
Chapter 68: "You shall not be overcome"
Chapter 73: Despair, depression, doubt, and fear

Chapters 80-81: Our life as penance and joy
Chapter 86: "Love was his meaning"

Julian's book received little notice until the twentieth century. But what has become the most noted work of Christian devotion is almost as old as hers, and we look next at that book and its writer – another friend.

7

MOST CLASSIC FRIEND

THOMAS À KEMPIS

The best-selling book in Christian history, apart from the Bible, is *The Imitation of Christ* by Thomas à Kempis. More than two thousand editions of it have been counted. Now available in over one hundred languages, it may have been read by as many as one billion people. With tear-filled eyes an experienced pastor said one day, "This is absolutely life-changing! I've never read anything like it." For many people it must be the most classic of friends. What is so great about this book which is now more than five hundred years old? And who was Thomas à Kempis?

He was born Thomas Haemerken in 1379 or 1380. His hometown was Kempen, near Dusseldorf and Cologne in present-day Germany. He felt called early to religious life, and his parents sent him to Deventer at the beginning of his teen years to further his education. At that time Deventer was the center for a renewal movement in the church known as the Modern Devotion (*Devotio moderna*) or Brethren of the Common Life. Founded by Gerard Groote (d. 1340), the movement called for genuine commitment to Christ, sincere love for God and neighbor, and ethical reform in the church. Although Groote did not require his followers to become monks, he did offer that possibility for those who wanted to do so. Having completed studies at Deventer, young Thomas applied in 1399 for admission to a new monastery of the Brethren near Zwolle. It was Mount St. Agnes, and his brother was its prior or administrative officer. He became known as Thomas à Kempis (from Kempen) and remained at Zwolle for most of his long life, until he died at ninety-one years of age.

Thomas progressed through the usual slow stages of monastic experience, receiving the monk's robe or habit, taking lifetime vows, and gaining ordination to the priesthood. He served the monastery as a copyist, laboring fifteen years to complete a Latin Bible for use in a church. Yet by the time he died, printing from moveable type had been invented and manuscript copyists were unemployed. After a quarter-century the community chose him in 1425 to be their sub-prior. In this capacity he was the novice master, instructing new recruits as well as those aspiring to monastic life. *The Imitation of Christ* apparently resulted from this activity, which in turn grew out of Thomas's own prolonged meditation on Christian life. He also may have had access to material from Gerard Groote, the founder of the *Devotio moderna*. If so, he edited that material, adapting and expanding it in his own way.

The monastery experienced troubled times in the 1420s, and the monks left Mount St. Agnes to go into voluntary exile, returning in 1432. Meanwhile Thomas's brother, now the superior in another monastic house, had become gravely ill. Thomas was allowed to go there and care for him until he died. Some years after the community had returned to Zwolle, Thomas again became its sub-prior (1448), remaining there until his death in 1471. The monks laid his body to rest in the east cloister of the monastery where his tomb remains to this day.

During his long life Thomas à Kempis wrote a number of books, but none of them approaches the value of *The Imitation of Christ*. Scholars have debated whether he actually wrote or simply edited the work, but all agree that he had the final word on its contents. Several manuscripts of the fifteenth-century book still exist, one of them signed by Thomas himself in 1441. This is one of the few books of Christian devotion honored by Catholics, Orthodox, and Protestants alike. That does not mean all agree on every point, but the good so predominates that its worth is unquestioned.

Ignatius Loyola, founder of the Jesuits, required members of the

Order to follow his practice and keep *The Imitation* with them at all times. Martin Luther held it in high regard, and it also influenced his opponent Erasmus of Rotterdam, who quoted from it in his last words. He in turn influenced the Anabaptists and Pietists of central Europe as well as England's John Wesley, who studied *The Imitation* carefully. Closer to our own day, when a plane crash in 1961 killed Dag Hammarskjöld, secretary-general of the United Nations, friends found his cherished copy of *The Imitation* on the nightstand next to his bed. And the revered nun Gavrilia (Gabriela, d. 1992), "the Orthodox Mother Teresa," treasured her own copy of Thomas à Kempis.

What is it about this little book that so moves, so inspires such a variety of readers? For one thing, its simplicity. Much of it, especially in the beginning, has the clipped, epigrammatic style of the book of Proverbs. Its overall biblical quality attracts, for it contains more than one thousand quotations and allusions to Christian scripture. Also, it challenges readers to meditate on Christ and imitate him, making this Christ-centeredness another of its attractions. It taps into what some have called the living core of Christian spirituality: an ongoing tradition of simplicity, obedience, and love which is both ascetical and mystical. We may find a final reason for its ongoing value in its summons to heroic commitment. Ordinary life calls for extraordinary action, however unnoticed, and *The Imitation* challenges all to consider and follow the naked Jesus.

Such language may sound harsh, but that was life in the monastery. Life today is also harsh, and the challenge Thomas penned for fellow monks speaks as well to other followers of Christ. Like Oswald Chambers in the twentieth century, he wants nothing less than "my utmost for His highest." To that end he addresses his readers in four books which originally circulated as separate booklets:

Book 1, "Counsels on the Spiritual Life," contains twenty-five chapters especially addressing the need for renunciation. Renounce the world, says Thomas. Renounce its materialism, classism, and pride. Think of others more highly than yourself. Cultivate discipline in prayer, thought, and speech. Commit yourself passionately to progress in your spiritual life.

Book 2, "Counsels on the Inner Life," consists of twelve chapters on how we can prepare to respond to God's work in us. Give first place to Christ in your heart is the challenge. Be inwardly united with his Spirit. Keep a clean conscience. See temptation as a means for growth. Don't try to avoid the cross – carry yours!

Book 3, with fifty-nine chapters, is by far the longest section. "On Inward Consolation" describes friendship with God, or what Thomas calls "love of Jesus." Pray to God with praise, thanksgiving, confession, and petition. Be a passionate follower of Christ. As William D. Longstaff reminds us in his classic hymn, "Take Time to Be Holy," "Speak oft' with your Lord. Abide in him always and feed on his Word." Fight the good fight – rebuke the devil! Take up the cross, not stoically but heroically.

The eighteen chapters of *Book 4,* "On the Blessed Sacrament," sum up earlier themes and bring them to a climax in eucharistic devotion. Do not approach the Lord's supper in either a rushed or relaxed manner – prepare yourself. Receive holy communion often. Remember God's grace through the gospel of Jesus Christ. Offer yourself totally to God.

The "counsels" given in *Book 1,* and to some extent in *Book 2,* may seem at first highly directive. Thomas almost sounds like a drill instructor addressing new recruits, which is what he was and did in the monastery. But in the life of faith we are all beginners, always. He speaks sternly because he knows sin's effects in human life are serious. When one arrives at *Book 3,* however, the style changes to become a series of conversations between the believer and Christ. The disciple, unworthy of grace, speaks to the gracious Lord who responds with acceptance and affirmation, encouragement and love. This climaxes in *Book 4* with its meditation on how in receiving holy communion we touch the living Christ. Threading their way through the four Books are repeated themes such as humility and self-denial (1.2), perseverance and courage (1.25), obedience and cross-bearing (2.11), what it means to fear and love God (3.2, 5), and what it means to meditate on Christ and imitate him (3.56).

The *Imitation* pulls no punches in identifying the believer's enemies – the world, the flesh, and the devil – and their impact on the life of the spirit. It challenges us to renounce anything that impedes our progress to Christ and embrace everything that brings us closer to him. It prays that we might become open, clean vessels to receive all he has for us. It begs for an immediacy of experience so close that, as Julian of Norwich said, there will be nothing between us and God. "O God, the Truth, make me one with you in endless love! I am often worn out by all that I read and hear; you are all that I want or desire. Let all teachers hold their peace. Let all creation be silent in your sight. You alone speak to me" (1.3, Creasy trans.).

The *Imitation of Christ* is in the Augustinian tradition which emphasizes the pervasiveness of sin, the resulting restlessness of the human heart, the grace of God, the sacrifice of Christ, the work of the Spirit in word, sacrament, and church, and the need for committed response in continuous self-offering. It is no wonder that a spiritual giant such as Baron Friedrich von Hugel devoted a quarter-hour every day for forty years to read and contemplate *The Confessions* of St. Augustine and *The Imitation of Christ*. Few who value those books would argue with such an investment of time.

In Thomas' Voice

Translations of the work of Thomas à Kempis exist in many languages, almost without number. One of the most attractive for contemporary readers is by UCLA professor William C. Creasy. From his expertise in fifteenth to seventeenth century devotional literature Creasy has attempted to reproduce in today's reader what the first readers of Thomas would have experienced more than five hundred years ago. The selections which follow are the words of Thomas from his translation *The Imitation of Christ: A Timeless Classic for Contemporary*

Readers, trans. by William C. Creasy (Notre Dame, IN: Ave Maria Press, 1989).

Be Watchful: Fire tempers iron, and temptation tempers the just person. Often, we do not know what we are able to do, but temptation reveals what we are. One must be watchful, however, especially when temptation begins, … for first a simple thought comes to the mind, and then a vivid picture takes shape; afterward comes delight, then a small mental concession, and finally ready acceptance. Thus, little by little, the malignant enemy gains full entrance when he is not resisted at the beginning. And the longer one puts off resisting, the weaker he becomes each day and the stronger the enemy grows (1.13).

God places more importance on the reason you work than on how much work you actually do (1.15).

We cannot trust ourselves too much, because we often lack grace and understanding…. Sometimes we are moved by passion and think it zeal. We condemn things in others and pass over serious things in ourselves…. You will never be inward and devout unless you stop talking about other people and start watching over yourself…. You will make great spiritual progress if you keep your nose out of other people's business; you will surely fail if you do not. Let nothing seem great, high, pleasing or agreeable to you, except God alone and what comes from God (2.5).

Praise does not make you holy; blame does not make you worthless (2.6).

A Friend of Jesus: You cannot live well without a friend, and if Jesus is not your best friend, you will end up being heartbroken and desolate. You act foolishly, then, if you center your life on anything else (2.8).

Grant me, most sweet and loving Jesus, to rest in you above every other creature, above all health and beauty, above all glory and honor, above all power and dignity, above all knowledge and precise thought, above all wealth and talent, above all joy and exultation, above all fame and praise, above all sweetness and consolation, above all hope and promise, above all merit and desire, above all gifts and favors you give and shower upon me, above all happiness and joy that the mind can understand and feel, and finally, above all angels and archangels, above all the hosts of heaven, above all things visible and invisible, and above all that is not you, my God (3.21).

My God and my all! What more can I want? What greater happiness can I desire? … My God and my all! Those words say enough to one who understands, but to one who loves, they are delightful to repeat over and over again (3.34).

Discernment: Grant me, Lord, to know what I ought to know, to love what I ought to love, to praise what is most pleasing to you, to esteem what seems most precious to you, to detest what is loathsome in your eyes. Let me not judge according to outward appearances nor condemn according to what people hear, but with true judgment let me discern between material and spiritual matters, and above all let me always seek to know your will (3.50).

All that must be radically overcome is rooted in this vice of making yourself the center of your own world (3.53).

Follow me. I am the Way, the Truth, and the Life. Without the Way, there is no going; without the Truth, there is no knowing; without the Life, there is no living. I am the Way you are to follow. I am the Truth you are to believe. I am the Life you are to hope for. I am the Way that cannot be destroyed, the Truth that cannot be wrong, the Life that cannot be ended. I am the Way that is most straight, the supreme Truth, the true Life, the blessed Life, begotten, not made (3.56).

The Weight of Your Cross: Lord Jesus, let it be as you have said and promised. Oh, that I may deserve it! I have shouldered the weight of your cross. I have taken it from your hands. You have placed it upon me, and I shall bear it, yes, even unto death. Truly, the life of a good monk – or of any good Christian – is a cross, but it is also his compass to paradise. Now that we have begun the journey, we must not go backward or give up.

So, come along! Let us go forward together! Jesus will be with us. For Jesus's sake we took up this cross; for Jesus's sake let us stick with it. Our Commander will be our helper. He has already scouted out the road. Look! our King marches ahead of us and will fight for us! Let us follow him courageously; let no one shrink at the terror! Let us be ready to die in battle! Let us not stain our glory by deserting the cross! (3.56).

If you feel yourself often set upon or badly tempted, still all is not lost. You are not God; you are a human being. You are flesh; you are not an angel (3.57).

Thomas's lifetime saw not only the invention of printing from movable type, but other significant changes as well. Constantinople, the capital of the Byzantine Empire, fell to Turkish forces in 1453. For a thousand years it had represented Christianity in southeastern Europe and the biblical lands. Christian scholars there fled into Europe, bringing with them manuscripts and knowledge unknown in the West. In Germany, Johann Gutenberg invented a process for printing from movable type – a technological revolution. Within another generation an Italian sailor named Columbus, financed by the Spanish monarchy, set foot in a new world across the Atlantic Ocean. And in 1483 a baby was born in Germany who would change Christian Europe forever.

8

NO LUTHERAN HE

MARTIN LUTHER

There is a story that five hundred years ago a German schoolmaster had an odd habit. When the day began, boys were expected to greet the teacher by removing their caps and bowing to him. It was a gesture of respect. But this teacher always reversed it – he removed his own cap and bowed to his pupils. When asked about this strange behavior, he had a simple reply: "Who knows? One of these boys might grow up to become a great man." Sitting in his class was a young pupil named Luder – Martin Luder – who later changed his name to Luther.

Whether the tale is true or not, Martin Luther did rise from humble beginnings to become one of the most influential figures in world history. So much has been written about him that it is difficult to describe his life briefly. He was born in Eisleben, Germany, southwest of Berlin, on November 10, 1483. The next year his parents, Hans and Margaretha Luder, moved to Mansfeld, where Hans worked in the copper mines. They dreamed that someday Martin would become a lawyer, get married, and make a lot of money. He attended school in several places and enjoyed music more than any other subject. Since he was skilled on both the flute and the lute, he sometimes played or sang in the streets for tuition money. Intending to please his parents, he studied law at the University of Erfurt, where he earned bachelor's and master's degrees. But during a severe thunderstorm in 1505, when he was almost struck by lightning, he changed his mind. Believing it was a sign from God who had spared his life, he vowed that he would become a monk – no law practice, no marriage, no money.

At twenty-one Luther entered the Order of Augustinian Hermits. He was ordained a priest three years later and said his first mass in the city of Wittenberg. It was clear that he was intellectually gifted, so with encouragement from his superiors he began to study toward a doctor's degree in theology. Having achieved that at twenty-nine, the monk now became a professor at the brand-new University of Wittenberg, where he lectured regularly on scripture. During his early thirties (1513-17), he especially studied and taught the books of Psalms, Romans, Galatians, and Hebrews. In them he found a message of salvation by God's grace rather than human effort, no matter how sincere. We can do nothing worthy of salvation; our lives can never merit God's goodness. Forgiveness is a gift which no amount of performance can merit or achieve. For Luther, this was a revolutionary message. This gospel, this good news – not church tradition – was the basis of Christian life, and the world needed to hear it.

Luther's world at the time was an exciting place. Major cities had emerged in Europe, many with universities, and they were a breeding ground of revolutionary ideas. Plato's spiritual, otherworldly philosophy had been largely eclipsed by Aristotle's here-and-now, this-world approach. An urban class of bankers and traders had risen to power. The papacy had peaked in the 1200s at the time of Francis of Assisi.

Christendom, understood as the mixture of politics and religion in Europe, had become shaky in the years since Francis. Constantinople, capital of the old Roman Empire in the East, fell to the Muslim Turks in 1453. Many of its scholars fled west into Europe, bringing with them both knowledge and precious manuscripts. About the same time a new technology exploded onto the scene when Johannes Gutenberg invented printing from movable type. Now anything could be duplicated quickly in affordable multiple copies. In 1492 an Italian sailor financed by the Spanish monarchy crossed the Atlantic, anchoring his ships in the Western hemisphere. And in several places distinguished scholars had begun to criticize the church's papal hierarchy as corrupt and its traditional theology as mistaken.

Young Dr. Luther was part of this new Europe. What he saw in the Catholic Church was out of step with what he had found in scripture. Church reform became the passion of his existence, and he was ready to join the discussion that already occupied many minds. So it is reported that on October 31, 1517, he followed the protocol of the day. At the church in Wittenberg he posted a list of ninety-five propositions he was prepared to debate with all comers. They were criticisms of the church, its hierarchy, and its theology. Ambitious printers quickly duplicated his theses, which circulated to great enthusiasm. Unknowingly he had ignited a fire which quickly became a conflagration.

Through the next two years he defended his ideas, insisting that the church's supreme authority is scripture – not popes or councils. The Catholic hierarchy wanted him sent to Rome for trial, but his prince, Frederick, known as the Wise, protected him from extradition. The year 1520 was especially significant. The pope gave Luther sixty days to retract what he had written or be declared a heretic. Luther received the order in October and responded sixty days later by burning it in public together with a pile of papal books. During that tumultuous year – sometimes called the watershed of the Reformation – he wrote three of his most important works: *To the Christian Nobility of the German Nation* (August), *The Babylonian Captivity of the Church* (October), and *The Freedom of a Christian* (November).

The first book challenged German princes and nobles to take the lead in reforming the church, since the pope would not lead the clergy to do so. The second, a more scholarly work, critiqued the church's approach to the sacraments. It had been carried captive, Luther argued, away from what scripture taught. He maintained that Christ had not ordained most of the traditional seven sacraments, and they should be demoted to a status below baptism and communion. The third book, more conciliatory and devotional in nature, discussed what it means to be free in Christ because of grace. Luther set out a double thesis: "A Christian is a perfectly free lord of all, subject to none. A Christian is a perfectly dutiful servant of all, subject to all" (*The Freedom of a Christian*). The pope responded by excommunicating him from the Catholic Church.

The die was cast. Luther the troublemaker was now summoned to appear in the city of Worms before the most powerful figure in the land, Charles V, Emperor of the Holy Roman Empire. During a tense confrontation, his opponents described him as a demon in the appearance of a man. Once more he refused to recant anything he had written. The verdict declared him to be a heretic and an outlaw, subject to arrest and execution. He was quickly seized, not by the authorities but by his friends. They spirited him away into a witness protection program. For almost a year he lived in hiding at the Wartburg Castle, home of Prince Frederick. During those months he grew a beard, wore civilian garb, and answered to the name Sir George. But he was not idle. He used his time and learning to translate the New Testament from the original Greek into German. He said he had never seen a Bible until he was twenty years old. Once he was freed, the possibility of arrest and execution would haunt him the rest of his life.

What followed began to shake Europe as Luther's sympathizers flocked to the cause of Christian liberty and church reform. In neighboring Switzerland followers of Ulrich Zwingli smashed stained glass windows and statues in their zeal to purify the church. The city of Geneva experienced significant, if severe, reform under the leadership of John Calvin. In England King Henry VIII declared that he, not the pope, was head of the church in that country. To the north John Knox thundered against the Catholic faith of Mary, Queen of Scots. And in several countries persecuted Anabaptists (rebaptizers) insisted that no one had yet gone far enough to reform the church along the lines of what Christ intended.

In Germany the energetic Luther, now out of hiding, continued his work, which had become many-sided. In 1525, at forty-one years of age, he broke his monastic vow of celibacy by taking a wife. Katharine von Bora was a feisty twenty-six-year-old former nun whom he hesitated to marry, fearing he would soon be killed. But their union lasted twenty years and gave them six children. One son died in infancy, and the death of thirteen-year-old Magdalena in 1542 broke her father's heart. But Kate, as Martin called his wife, turned out to be an excellent companion and manager. The Augustinian monastery where he had lived as a monk was given to them, and she turned it into a virtual motel. She adroitly managed the busy household of her husband, their children, the farm which supported them, and the many visitors who came to their door for discussion or refuge.

Luther himself was occupied with trying to guide the Reformation movement. He preached almost every day, wrote theological tracts, produced biblical commentaries, developed orders of worship, and continued to translate the Bible. It is said that he wrote or dictated the equivalent of three hundred books of two hundred pages each. The complete writings of his lifetime in their latest English version amount to fifty-five printed volumes. His friend and lieutenant Philip Melancthon did not deny Luther's violent, even coarse language in attacking the church system of the time. When giving Luther's funeral oration, Melancthone defended Luther in the words of their contemporary, Erasmus: "Because of the magnitude of the disorders, God gave this age a violent physician." But Luther also could be charming with friends and tender with his family. His devotional, personal side shows through especially in *The Freedom of the Christian* and *Table Talk* — friends' reminiscences of mealtime conversations.

For a quarter-century the turmoil raged. Politics and economics were involved along with the religious ferment. In the end, much of what we call Germany became Lutheran along with most of Scandinavia. Nations east, west and south of Germany (modern Poland, France, Spain, and Italy) remained Catholic. To the north, England and Scotland broke with the papacy, while Ireland remained loyal to Rome. Farther to the east, Russia had been Orthodox for five hundred years, but the Muslim Turks were always a threat to the West.

Luther suffered from a long list of health problems and was sometimes ill for months at a time. Although Kate was a skilled herbalist, excruciating headaches, kidney-stone attacks, and bouts of depression wracked him. Still, he plunged on in spite of energies that inevitably waned. He was sixty-two years of age when he died on February 18, 1546, in Eisleben, the town of his birth. Friends and followers took his body to Wittenberg, where his public career had begun, and there they laid him to rest. Katharine lived another six years, dying in 1552. Today some consider Martin Luther to be the second most significant figure in Western Christianity since the apostles. He would be pleased to know that first place goes to his theological mentor, Augustine of Hippo.

In Luther's Voice

Luther once remarked that he could wish all his books would perish if only people would read the Bible. He wanted no one to be called a Lutheran – his followers were to be Christians only. He believed that his two best works were *The Bondage of the Will* (1525) and *The Small Catechism* (1529). The first was a scholarly defense of human sinfulness and divine grace. The second – much more personal – contains a short exposition of the Ten Commandments, the Apostles' Creed, and the Lord's Prayer in question-and-answer format. Luther wrote it for parents to use in teaching their children the elements of Christian faith. Here is the section of Luther's thoughts on the Creed. It deserves to be read with care, pondering each phrase. Notice how simply, personally, and concretely Luther explains the basics of Christian belief.

The First Article: Creation

"I believe in God, the Father almighty, maker of heaven and earth."

What does this mean?
   Answer: I believe that God has created me and all that exists; that he has given me and still sustains my body and soul, all my limbs and senses, my reason and all the faculties of my mind, together with food and clothing, house and home, family and property; that he provides

me daily and abundantly with all the necessities of life, protects me from all danger, and preserves me from all evil. All this he does out of his pure, fatherly, and divine goodness and mercy, without any merit or worthiness on my part. For all of this I am bound to thank, praise, serve, and obey him. This is most certainly true.

The Second Article: Redemption

"And in Jesus Christ, his only son, our Lord: who was conceived by the Holy Spirit, born of the virgin Mary, suffered under Pontius Pilate, was crucified, dead, and buried: he descended into hell, the third day he rose from the dead, he ascended into heaven, and is seated on the right hand of God, the Father almighty, whence he shall come to judge the living and the dead."

What does this mean?

Answer: I believe that Jesus Christ, true God, begotten of the Father from eternity, and also true man, born of the virgin Mary, is my Lord, who has redeemed me, a lost and condemned creature, delivered me and freed me from all sins, from death, and from the power of the devil, not with silver and gold but with his holy and precious blood and with his innocent sufferings and death, in order that I may be his, live under him in his kingdom, and serve him in everlasting righteousness, innocence, and blessedness, even as he is risen from the dead and lives and reigns to all eternity. This is most certainly true.

The Third Article: Sanctification

"I believe in the Holy Spirit, the holy Christian church, the communion of saints, the forgiveness of sins, the resurrection of the body, and the life everlasting. Amen."

What does this mean?

Answer: I believe that by my own reason or strength I cannot believe in Jesus Christ, my Lord, or come to him. But the Holy Spirit has called me through the Gospel, enlightened me with his gifts, and sanctified and preserved me in the true faith, just as he calls, gathers, enlightens, and sanctifies the whole Christian church on earth and preserves it in union with Jesus Christ in the one true faith. In this Christian church he daily and abundantly forgives all my sins, and the sins of all believers, and on the last day he will raise me and all the dead and will grant eternal life to me and to all who believe in Christ. This is most certainly true [Denis Janz, *Three Reformation Catechisms: Catholic, Anabaptist, Lutheran* (New York: Edwin Mellen Press, 1982), p. 193ff.].

Apart from his contributions to theology, Luther gave the church two other great gifts: the Bible in German and the hymnal. For about a thousand years, music in worship had been the province of clergy and choirs, but the Reformer insisted that all Christians must be free to sing. He even scheduled rehearsals for congregations to practice hymn-singing! Because of this, some have estimated that by 1600 Germany had produced twenty thousand hymns – more than any other country – some by Luther himself. Without question, "A Mighty Fortress Is Our God" ranks as the most famous hymn Luther wrote. He adapted the text from Psalm 46 and also composed the music. It reflects the danger of the time in which he lived and his courage in facing it. Here it is in the popular translation of Frederick H. Hedge (1852).

A Hymn

A mighty Fortress is our God,
A bulwark never failing;
Our Helper He amid the flood
Of mortal ills prevailing:
For still our ancient foe
Doth seek to work us woe;
His craft and power are great,
And, armed with cruel hate,
On earth is not his equal.

Did we in our own strength confide,
Our striving would be losing;
Were not the right Man on our side,
The Man of God's own choosing:
Dost ask who that may be?
Christ Jesus, it is He;
Lord Sabaoth His name,
From age to age the same,
And He must win the battle.

And though this world, with devils filled,
Should threaten to undo us;
We will not fear, for God hath willed
His truth to triumph through us:
The Prince of Darkness grim,
We tremble not for him;
His rage we can endure,
For lo! His doom is sure,
One little word shall fell him.

That word above all earthly power,
No thanks to them, abideth;
The Spirit and the gifts are ours
Through Him who with us sideth:
Let goods and kindred go,
This mortal life also;
The body they may kill;
God's truth abideth still,
His Kingdom is forever.

Martin Luther prayed a great deal – his contentious career demanded it. Here is an example of a very personal, intimate prayer.

A Prayer

Behold, Lord, an empty vessel that needs to be filled. My Lord, fill it. I am weak in the faith; strengthen thou me. I am cold in love; warm me and make me fervent that my love may go out to my neighbour. I do not have a strong and firm faith; at times I doubt and am unable to trust thee altogether. O Lord, help me. Strengthen my faith and trust in thee. In thee I have sealed the treasures of all I have. I am poor; thou art rich and didst come to be merciful to the poor. I am a sinner; thou art upright. With me there is an abundance of sin; in thee is the fullness of righteousness. Therefore, I will remain with thee of whom I can receive but to whom I may not give. Amen. [*The Oxford Book of Prayer*, ed. by George Appleton (New York: Oxford University Press, 1985), p. 53].

Luther is reported to have said that, when it came to reforming the church, he merely lit the fire which others before him had prepared. As the Protestant Reformation began to change the church in western Europe, the Catholics did some reforming as well. It came especially in some of the monastic Orders, and one of the greatest reformers was a woman.

9

MYSTIC AND MANAGER

TERESA OF AVILA

What is in the mind of a young girl who wants to be killed so she can see Jesus? Clearly, she has learned something early, but there is also childish confusion. That was the experience of one of Christendom's most honored saints, Teresa of Avila. Her hometown, Avila, lies in central Spain northwest of Madrid. There Teresa de Cepeda y Ahumada was born in 1515 into an old, well-to-do family. She grew up in the years when the Reformation started by Martin Luther was agitating northern Europe and Great Britain, but the countries of Latin culture (Spain, France, and Italy) remained faithful to Roman Christianity led by the pope. It was a time when Spain was a superpower, much of it due to exploration and conquest in the New World.

When Teresa was seven years old, she and her brother ran away from home, hoping to become martyrs and thus see Jesus. Thankfully, their plot failed and they were returned to their parents. Teresa was an attractive, intelligent girl who became quite an adolescent flirt with the boys in Avila. She also had an intense, serious side and at twenty-one, against her father's wishes, entered the Carmelite Order to become a nun. The Carmelites, then five hundred years old, had begun with a few hermits living on Mount Carmel in the Holy Land. From there they moved into Europe where they became a well-known monastic Order.

Two years into her life as a nun Teresa nearly died in an illness where she experienced a special closeness to Jesus in prayer. She recovered, although with intermittent paralysis of her legs, and continued as a Carmelite. But for about seventeen years she wavered in what she considered lax spiritual practice. Although the Order had begun with strict ideals of poverty, fasting, and solitude, by the mid-1500s it had become an easy-going, popular institution with lax discipline.

When Teresa was forty, she experienced what she called a second conversion, one that was both mystical and practical. Those two traits would mark the rest of her life. She could have exalted mystical experiences in prayer and also be a down-to-earth, hands-on manager. Convinced that her Order needed to be reformed, after considerable pleading she got permission in 1562 to found a new, stricter convent in Avila. However, nuns in an existing convent and citizens of the town opposed the plan. A lawsuit followed but was finally settled, and by year's end Teresa and the sisters with her had returned to the disciplined practice of the Order's early years. They would be known as Discalced Carmelites; that is, those who went barefoot or wore only sandals rather than shoes or boots. But resistance continued and would plague her efforts the rest of her life. These impoverished, unshod nuns were going too far!

Teresa's ever-watchful superiors ordered her to write her autobiography, which she did as an act of obedience. She called it simply *The Story of My Life*. It was carefully scrutinized by the Inquisition, now in its most intense period of activity. Ferdinand and Isabella, the monarchs who financed Columbus's voyages to the New World, had established the Inquisition in Spain. Although in existence for many years in various countries, its Spanish form was the most terrifying of all. With full state approval, church authorities had sweeping power to arrest suspected heretics, interrogate, torture, and condemn them to death by burning. Several thousand people, many undoubtedly innocent, perished in this way. Was Teresa guilty of heresy? Her beliefs were orthodox, but she was walking a fine line in her efforts to produce a more pure monastic life. Her opponents were many, and they were strong.

Teresa managed to escape condemnation and summarized her life story in *The Way of Perfection*, which she wrote for her discalced sisters. About this time she met a small young priest, also a Carmelite, who went by the name Juan de la Cruz (John of the Cross). Born in 1542, he was twenty-seven years her junior, but she recognized in him a mind and spirit akin to her own. Unlike her, he was born into poverty, but his intelligence and maleness prevailed to get him an excellent university education. She persuaded him to join the Discalced Carmelites, and together they founded two new monasteries for the renewal. Now there were houses for both men and women in the emerging reformed wing of the Carmelite Order.

For the next fifteen years Teresa and John traveled and labored throughout Spain to foster their reformation of Catholic practice among the Carmelites. Theirs is one of the most outstanding spiritual partnerships of all time. They were classic friends in the best sense. She could even joke that because John was so short, God had sent her only half a priest! Teresa established seventeen more convents, but she experienced inconsistent support from her superiors, tension within the larger Order, and inquiries from the Inquisition. She was in constant danger on all three fronts. During this time her superiors again ordered her to write – this time her ideas on prayer. At age sixty-two, between June and November 1577, working at high speed along with all her other responsibilities, Teresa produced what became her spiritual masterpiece, *The Interior Castle*.

Meanwhile, John of the Cross was imprisoned in 1577 by the Calced Carmelites who placed him in solitary confinement. They treated him with savage harshness, but he managed to escape. He went on to write a handful of poetic masterpieces in which he described and analyzed in his own way the soul's experience as it progresses in prayer. By 1580 the separation between the two wings of the Order was final. John continued to be active in higher education and directed monasteries among the Discalced Carmelites until he incurred the wrath of his own superiors. He was banished, became seriously ill, was refused medical treatment, and died after great suffering in 1591 at the age of forty-nine.

He had outlived Teresa by almost ten years, composing some of the most beautiful lyric poetry in the Spanish language. He wrote four books which are explanations and commentaries on his poems: *The Ascent of Mount Carmel*, *The Dark Night*, *The Spiritual Canticle*, and *The Living Flame of Love*. They are treasured for their description and analysis of the deeper, higher reaches of prayer.

Teresa founded her last monastic house in 1582 under great difficulties and then fell ill. She died at the age of sixty-seven on October 4, the feast day of the earlier reformer Francis of Assisi. Her life had been one of constant activity, shrewd administration, ecstatic transports in prayer, and frequent danger. Almost four hundred years later she received the highest honor the Catholic Church can give. In 1970 Pope Paul VI proclaimed her, like Bernard of Clairvaux, a Doctor of the church – an exceptional, exemplary teacher for all of Christendom. Only about thirty people have been so honored, and Teresa of Avila was the first woman to be included among them.

She remains to this day one of the most attractive, courageous figures in the church's history. Although she opposed the Protestant Reformation as she knew it, she gave her life to reform the Catholic Church. Active as a superintending administrator in her Order, she was also a mystic who wrote in the language of the people. Always faithful to her church, she was under its constant suspicion and often in danger. Plagued by ill health, she still managed arduous journeys and negotiations to follow her calling. She was a woman of great intelligence, perseverance, courage, wit, wisdom, and faith. Today her books are studied by scholars and enjoyed by thousands of readers around the world.

In Teresa's Voice

Teresa could be very modest when it came to her writings. Was it genuine humility, or was she adopting the role expected of women at that time? Was she downplaying her own insight and experience to escape the wrath of her superiors? No one knows for sure, but here are some comments she made to a priest friend about her writing:

On Writing. Why do they want me to write things? Let learned men, who have studied, do the writing. I am a stupid creature and don't know what I am saying. There are more than enough books written on prayer already. For the love of God, let me get on with my spinning and go to choir and do my religious duties like the other sisters. I am not meant for writing. I have neither the health nor the wits for it.

The Spanish cities and countryside were dotted with castles, many of them built by the Moors, Muslims from North Africa who had lived peacefully in Spain until Ferdinand and Isabella expelled them. Teresa knew these castles had gated walls with various buildings inside them, all surrounding a central tower where the castle's lord and his family lived. *The Interior Castle* by Teresa pictures the soul as a castle in which prayer moves from outside to inside, through ascending levels (mansions), until in the highest experience there could be a spiritual marriage with the Lord. The book survived scrutiny to become a world-famous text on the progress of inner prayer.

Here are two selections of Teresa's words from the well-known translation by E. Allison Peers [Image Books. (New York: Doubleday, 1989)].

The Interior Castle It is very important that no soul which practices prayer, whether little or much, should be subjected to undue constraint or limitation. Since God has given it such dignity, it must be allowed to roam through these mansions – through those above, those below and those on either side. It must not be compelled to remain for a long time in one single room — not, at least, unless it is in the room of self-knowledge. . . . However high a state the soul may have attained, self-knowledge is incumbent upon it, and this it will never be able to neglect even should it so desire. Humility must always be doing its work like a bee making its honey in the hive: without humility all will be lost. Still, we should remember that the bee is constantly flying about from flower to flower, and in the same way, believe me, the soul must sometimes emerge from self-knowledge and soar aloft in meditation upon the greatness and the majesty of its God....

I do not know if I have explained this clearly: self-knowledge is so important that, even if you were raised right up to the heavens, I should like you never to relax your cultivation of it; so long as we are on this earth, nothing matters more to us than humility. . . . As I see it, we shall never succeed in knowing ourselves unless we seek to know God [from First Mansions, p. 37f.].

. . . the important thing is not to think much, but to love much; do, then, whatever most arouses you to love . . . . For love consists, not in the extent of our happiness, but in the firmness of our determination to try to please God in everything" [from Fourth Mansions, p. 76].

Teresa's Bookmark is the name given to the following words found after her death on a bookmark in her prayerbook.

> Let nothing disturb thee;
> Let nothing dismay thee;
> All things pass;
> God never changes.
> Patience attains
> All that it strives for.
> He who has God
> Finds he lacks nothing:
> God alone suffices

[quoted from Richard J. Woods, *Christian Spirituality: God's Presence through the Ages* (Maryknoll, NY: Orbis Books, rev. ed., 2006), p. 208].

As we have seen in Teresa's life, she was both mystical and practical in her approach to faith. Our next friend, Brother Lawrence, was nothing if not practical in his service to God and his example of a natural relationship with his heavenly Father.

10

A STUDY IN CAREER CHANGE

BROTHER LAWRENCE

Career changes happen all the time in our day. Even those who stay in one job often need retraining because of new developments. Most college students will switch majors at least once before they graduate. These changes are not unique to the twenty-first century, as Christian history includes examples of career changes from bygone eras. One of the most interesting is the story of Nicolas Herman, better known as Lawrence of the Resurrection or just plain Brother Lawrence.

He was born in 1611 or 1614 in Lorraine, an area between France and Germany which belonged at that time to France. Unlike Germany, France had remained Catholic when the Protestant Reformation occurred. Nicolas grew up in a pious Catholic home, received rudimentary schooling, and soon went off to the army. What history calls the Thirty Years' War had begun in 1618 and would conclude only in 1648. The issue was whether the land should be Catholic or some variety of Protestant, and the struggle was savage. The civilian population suffered terribly as year after year armies rampaged back and forth destroying towns, burning crops, and brutalizing the people.

Nicolas served in the French army and was taken prisoner. The Germans thought he was a spy and threatened to hang him, but his simple manner convinced them he was harmless. Amazingly, they sent him back to his own army. Later, in a battle against Swedish troops, he received a serious leg wound and was allowed to return home to recuperate. But the recovery was incomplete, forcing him to walk all his life with a pronounced limp.

When he was eighteen (before or during his military service – we don't know), he experienced a religious conversion. As he reported it, he noticed a bare tree in midwinter. Knowing the tree would come to life in the spring, he applied the idea to himself. Believing God loved him as well as the tree, Nicolas opened his heart, asking God to give him new life like the tree.

When he could no longer engage in military service, he changed careers. He became a servant in the household of a nobleman who was the king's treasurer. The king of France at the time was Louis XIV, the Sun King, who built the famed palace at Versailles. But Nicolas was clumsy by nature, which his war wound made only worse, and he kept breaking his employer's valuable possessions. So he was fired, another unwelcome change. His time in military and domestic service amounted to about eighteen years. Wanting his life to belong wholly to God, he tried living as a hermit – but that didn't work for him either. Finally a relative suggested that he try getting into a monastery. There he could live out God's call on his life in a community of like-minded men where he would find support and accountability. This would be his vocation for the rest of his life.

In 1642 Nicolas was allowed to enter a monastery of the Discalced Carmelites in Paris. The monks spent much time in prayer and meditation along the lines set out by their founders, Teresa of Avila and John of the Cross. Nicolas proceeded through the stages of admission until he became an accepted lay brother with the name Lawrence of the Resurrection. He never advanced to the priesthood, however, but always remained just Brother Lawrence, one among the lowest group in the community. Founded in 1611, part of that extensive monastery has survived four hundred years and is still in existence today.

At first Brother Lawrence found the structured prayers and confessions to be difficult, for his spirit craved a more natural, spontaneous approach to God. Later he made no secret of how hard that time was. But he persevered for ten years following the monastic rule, and then he had a breakthrough. Throwing himself on God's mercy, he told the Father that he would love him even if he were sent to hell. From then on, Brother Lawrence experienced an inner peace beyond anything he could describe. He also realized that outside the hours set for designated prayers he could pray as he wished. So on his own time he began to carry on a silent conversation with God, speaking personally and openly. He was a simple man, and he talked to God simply and frankly. He called it "the practice of the presence of God." He tried to think of God in each moment and do everything assigned to him out of love for God, not just obedience to his superiors.

Lay brothers were expected to pray and do manual labor. Brother Lawrence's assignment was kitchen duty. He was a cook for the monastery, trying in its busy kitchen to do each thing in sequence for the love of God. With sometimes more than one hundred men to feed, this was no easy task. Occasionally the monastery sent him a long distance by riverboat to restock their wine supply. This made him nervous because he was not confident of handling all the transactions well, and his leg bothered him a lot. It was so bad that on deck he could move around best by rolling himself from one barrel to another. But he accepted the assignment as from God, asking his assistance to complete it, and at the end thanked him gratefully. He spent fifteen years in kitchen duty with its various responsibilities.

Word began to get out that there was a special man in the monastery, a man close to God, a holy man. It was not the abbot in charge or his assistant, the prior – it was the cook, plain Brother Lawrence. Monks and nuns in other places began writing to him, and an important priest interviewed him several times in 1666-67. Outwardly he seemed rather crusty and brusque, but the priest soon recognized the cook's genuine, tender heart. His basic teaching about how to love God ran along the line of the famous K.I.S.S. formula – "Keep it simple, stupid!" Meanwhile, as his leg continued to deteriorate, he was relieved of kitchen duty and assigned to the cobbler's shop. There he could sit while working to create or repair the sandals which the monks wore. Eventually his leg became diseased and ulcerated. Brother Lawrence suffered greatly but bravely until his spirit slipped away on February 12, 1691.

Following his death, those who loved him began to exchange the letters he had written to them. The next year the priest who had interviewed him published his notes from their conversations together with letters and other materials he had collected. But it was not a good time for that. French Catholic leaders were embroiled in a controversy over "quietism" (a totally passive approach to prayer), and some of them thought what Brother Lawrence said sounded like that. Although many appreciated his simple, direct teaching based on the love of God, it was swept away and forgotten.

But in England people began to notice his approach as they read it in the original French. Then in 1724 *The Practice of the Presence of God* appeared in an English translation. From that time until now, multitudes have read and honored Brother Lawrence as a classic devotional writer. Orthodox nun Gavrilia held him in high regard along with Thomas à Kempis. Among Protestants, Hannah Whitall Smith authored one of the nineteenth century's most popular devotional books, *The Christian's Secret of a Happy Life*. She called Brother Lawrence's work "one of the most helpful books I know…. It fits into the lives of all human beings." Hal Helms, who edited a recent translation of *The Practice of the Presence of God*, said of Brother Lawrence, "We understand him and love him for his realistic honesty."

Realism, bluntness, candor, honesty — such down-to-earth traits have endeared the simple monk to thousands of readers. His sense of God's care and closeness is inviting. The brevity of his writings, the shortest of all devotional classics, is attractive. (The whole *Practice of the Presence of God* can be printed in a booklet slim enough to fit shirt-pocket or purse without a bulge.) Although never honored by his church, Brother Lawrence continues to bless us today. His love for God and his message to keep our love simple remain his gifts to the church.

In Brother Lawrence's Voice

The material by and about Brother Lawrence was originally collected and published by the Abbé Joseph de Beaufort, the priest who interviewed him. It exists today in a variety of English translations. An especially attractive version is by Robert J. Edmonson in the Christian Classics Living Library (Brewster, MA: Paraclete Press, 1985). The most famous passage from Brother Lawrence may be this one:

In My Kitchen "The time of business," he used to say, "is no different from the time of prayer. I possess God as tranquilly in the noise and clatter of my kitchen, where sometimes several people ask me different things at the same time, as if I were on my knees before the Blessed Sacrament."

After Brother Lawrence died, the Abbé de Beaufort managed to collect sixteen of the monk's letters. The one believed to be earliest is dated 1682, while he wrote the last one just six days before he died in 1691. But most of the letters are undated and their recipients are unknown. Here is a letter Brother Lawrence wrote to an unnamed woman.

To an Unknown Woman. [God] does not require a great deal of us; all He asks is a little remembrance of Him from time to time, a little worship. Sometimes we should ask for His grace, and sometimes we should offer Him our sufferings. At other times we ought to thank Him for the grace He has given us and which He is working in us.

In the midst of your work console yourself with Him as often as you can. During your meals and your conversations, lift your heart towards Him from time to time; the slightest little remembrance will always be very pleasant to Him. To do this you do not need to shout out loud. He is closer to us than we think.

We do not have to be constantly in church to be with God. We can make our heart a prayer room into which we can retire from time to time to converse with Him gently, humbly and lovingly. Everyone is capable of these conversations with God – some more, some less. He knows what our capabilities are. Let us begin, for perhaps He is only awaiting a generous resolve on our part. Take courage, for we have little time left to live. You are almost sixty-four years old, and I am approaching eighty. Let us live and die with God! Our sufferings will always be sweeter and more pleasant when we are with Him, and without Him, our greatest pleasure will be but a cruel torture.

So make it a habit little by little to worship Him in this way. Ask Him for His grace and offer Him your heart from time to time during the day in the midst of your work – at every moment if you are able. Do not constrain yourself by rules or private devotions. Offer Him your heart in faith, with love and humility [*The Practice of the Presence of God*, trans. by Robert J. Edmonson (Brewster, MA: Paraclete Press, rev. ed., 1985), p. 89f.].

Thank you, Brother Lawrence. As we move into the seventeenth century, our next friend shows another example of a heart committed to God, even though he was often imprisoned. In fact, John Bunyan's *Pilgrim's Progress*, still cherished today, was penned while in jail.

11

JAILHOUSE NOVELIST

JOHN BUNYAN

How can a man with almost no education write a book that becomes a world-famous best seller? That in a nutshell is the story of John Bunyan, author of *The Pilgrim's Progress*. For three hundred years after its publication in 1678, it was the most famous Protestant book in the English language. But the adventure story it relates is no more exciting than the life of its author.

John Bunyan lived from 1628 to 1688, in one of the most tumultuous periods in English history. A hundred years earlier King Henry VIII broke with the papacy in Rome, declaring himself – not the pope – head of the church in England. Three of his children succeeded him, and in their reigns the nation's leadership swung from Protestant to Catholic and, with Queen Elizabeth I, to a somewhat middle position. Many churchmen (Puritans) hoped to purify the official Church of England along more Protestant lines and create a model society governed by their understanding of the Bible. However, King James I and his son Charles I, believing they had a divine right to govern alone, fought with Parliament and at times ruled without it. This led to civil war in 1642 and the execution of King Charles in 1649. About thirty thousand Puritans separated from the established church and emigrated to New England. And sometime in 1628 John Bunyan was born at Elstow near Bedford, north of London.

He learned to read and write in the village school and intended to follow his father's trade as a tinker, mending pots and pans. But in his middle teens his world collapsed. When he was fifteen his mother died in June, his sister died in July, and in August his father remarried. The next year his larger world also collapsed as England's civil war began. Sixteen-year-old John was drafted into the Parliamentary (Puritan) army where he served for three years. When the monarchy was overthrown in 1649, the victorious Puritans established in its place a commonwealth.

Bunyan was allowed to return home where he began to work as a tinker. At twenty he married a godly wife who bore four children in the years that followed. Sadly, we do not know her name. But it was customary to give the first daughter her mother's name, and Bunyan's eldest daughter was called Mary. As the family grew and his wife influenced him more and more, Bunyan thought seriously about who he was, what he was about, and where he was headed. He had been christened as a baby, but at twenty-five he was baptized in Bedford's Nonconformist (independent) church, and soon afterward began to preach and write. Despite his scant formal education, he knew the Bible so well that people called him a walking concordance. His facility with English was so good that he became a popular, well-known preacher.

His wife died when he was twenty-nine, and two years later he remarried. His second wife, Elizabeth, was also a godly woman, and they had two children together. Times grew harder as the commonwealth collapsed and the Catholic monarchy returned in 1660. Now, with the Act of Uniformity (1662), Puritanism was suppressed. All clergy who did not obey the new rules were ejected from their parishes. John Bunyan was of an independent mind and belonged to an independent church. He refused to let the state dictate his ministry, so between the ages of thirty-two and forty-nine he was in and out of jail for twelve years. He served two six-year terms plus several shorter sentences.

Jail for Bunyan was difficult but not desperate. At times the jailer would release him for the weekend, knowing that John would go into the countryside to preach. When word spread that Bunyan was out and intended to preach, people flocked to hear him. Then, when all was finished, he faithfully returned to the jail where he was locked up again. Elizabeth and their daughter Mary often visited him, especially to bring a pot of soup. Although Mary was blind, she knew the route so well that sometimes she went alone through the streets to the jail. Bunyan said the hardest trial of his imprisonment was being away from his family, especially his blind daughter, but she and Elizabeth were as committed to the cause as he was.

During these stretches in jail, he made shoelaces to help support the family, and he wrote. At age thirty-eight he published his autobiography, *Grace Abounding to the Chief of Sinners*. At fifty, using his fertile imagination and his knowledge of the Bible, Bunyan finished a novel, *The Pilgrim's Progress from This World to That Which Is to Come* (1678). It tells the story of Christian, who escapes the City of Destruction and through many adventures makes his way to the Celestial City. In his journey he meets an intriguing cast of characters such as Mr. Worldly-Wiseman, Judge Hate-good, the giant Despair, Ignorance, and Talkative. Christian is misunderstood, attacked, and jailed but pushes on with determination.

When he wavers, God sends companions Faithful and Hopeful to accompany and encourage him. Bunyan peppers the plot with long conversations in which Christian argues against all comers for his understanding of salvation. And the book is generously salted with biblical quotations on almost every page. But novels were a novelty among the Puritans, and Bunyan had to make a case for writing Christian fiction. Not all imagination, he maintained, is of the devil.

At last John Bunyan was released from jail and became pastor of the Independent church in Bedford. He preached widely but declined to move away from the village he had called home all his life. Along with preaching and caring for his congregation he managed to write a number of other books; for example, Part Two of *The Pilgrim's Progress*. This story never caught on like the earlier one, and today people usually mean only the first part when they refer to *The Pilgrim's Progress*. Among his other noted works were *The Life and Death of Mister Badman* and a long allegory, *The Holy War*.

In the summer of 1688 Bunyan rode south in heavy rain to preach in London. There he became ill and died on August 31. He was fifty-nine. Elizabeth lived another three years, dying at about the age of sixty in 1691. Their lives coincided with the period when the monarchy and the Church of England suppressed those who would not conform to their dictates. One year after Bunyan's death the Act of Toleration (1689) halted suppression of Puritans and all other Christians who might be called Dissenters.

Bunyan was buried in London's Bunhill Fields Cemetery, which later welcomed other Nonconformists such as John and Charles Wesley's mother Susanna and Isaac Watts, the father of English hymnody. But Bunyan's greatest monument is *The Pilgrim's Progress* with its portrayal of Christian life as a journey full of adventure and danger, a journey which demands discipline, endurance, and courage. We are on a pilgrimage to the holy city, the new Jerusalem, and the journey calls for perseverance to the very end.

In Bunyan's Voice

John Bunyan wrote *The Pilgrim's Progress* about sixty years after the King James Version Bible was published. Like the Bible, some of its later editions have updated the language in keeping with changing styles of English. One good version is *The New Pilgrim's Progress* with revised text by Judith E. Markham.

Christian's progress from the City of Destruction to the Celestial City is filled with danger. Along the way he meets fellow pilgrim Faithful who later is killed for his outspoken witness to Christ. Christian then encounters Hopeful, and they travel together until at last they reach the Celestial City. Here is a condensed version of how the story ends. As in all Bunyan's writings, echoes of the Bible and its language abound.

The Celestial City. Christian and Hopeful were met by two men in garments that shone like gold; also their faces shone like light. They went on together until they came within sight of the gate. Now I noticed that between them and the gate was a river, but there was no bridge across it. Then they asked the men if the waters were all of the same depth. They said, 'No,' but they could not help them with that. 'For,' they said, 'you will find it deeper or shallower, according to your faith in the King of the place.'

They waded into the water, and Christian began to sink, crying out, 'I sink in deep waters; the billows go over my head; all his waves go over me! Selah.' Then Hopeful said, 'Have courage, my brother, for I feel the bottom, and it is solid.' And with that a great darkness and horror fell upon Christian so that he could not see before him. Everything he said focused on his terrible fears. Then said Hopeful, 'These troubles you are going through in these waters are not a sign that God has forsaken you. They are sent to try you. They test whether you will remember all his previous mercy to you and rely on him in your distress.' Then they took courage, and thus they crossed over.

Now as they drew near the gate, a company of the heavenly host came out to meet them. Several of the King's trumpeters also came out; it was as if heaven itself had come down to meet them. They could see the city itself now, and they thought they heard all the bells ringing to welcome them. Christian and Hopeful went through the gate; and as they entered, they were transfigured. They had garments put on them that shone like gold. Then all the bells in the city rang again for joy, and they were told, 'Enter into the joy of your Lord.' I also heard the men themselves singing with a loud voice, 'Blessing, honor, glory, and power be to the one seated upon the throne, and to the Lamb, for ever and ever.' And I awoke, and behold it was a dream [*The New Pilgrim's Progress,* revised text by Judith E. Markham (Grand Rapids: Discovery House Publishers, 1989), pp. 210-219, abridged and altered].

The century following Bunyan's death was the Age of Reason, when the universe was considered to be a machine, and everything could be explained in terms of human thinking. Churches and their leaders could often become cold and rationalistic, left-brained we might say today. But the human heart cries out for something more, and in England that cry was answered in a nationwide revival movement led by two graduates of Oxford University.

12

METHODICAL BROTHERS

JOHN AND CHARLES WESLEY

When there are nineteen children in a family, life will either be organized or chaotic. The Wesley household of eighteenth-century England was organized, principally because Mrs. Wesley was both a disciplinarian and a manager. Life also was sad because half of the children died in infancy. Of sturdy Puritan stock, Susanna Wesley could read several languages and home-schooled the children six hours each day. Her husband, the Reverend Samuel Wesley, was the Anglican priest in charge of the parish of Epworth, north of London. No Puritan, he was of the High-Church party, a strong and passionate supporter of the monarchy.

John, their fifteenth child, was born in 1703, followed in four years by his brother Charles, the eighteenth. Life went along pretty much as expected in the Wesley family until one night in 1709 when their house caught fire. It took only minutes for the thatched roof to be engulfed in flames. With the help of neighbors everyone got out of the building -- or so they thought. To their horror they saw six-year-old John standing at an open upstairs window, fire already in the room. With not a moment to lose, the men on hand formed a human ladder up the side of the house. The man on top snatched John out of the window and lowered him safely to the ground. For the rest of his long life John Wesley considered himself "a brand plucked from the burning," and it fired his evangelistic zeal.

Samuel and Susanna had some differing ideas. He was often out of town, so in his absence Susanna began teaching Bible classes on Sunday afternoon. When attendance at her Bible studies outgrew his Sunday morning services, Samuel ordered her to stop. She replied that she would not. God had asked her to begin, she said, and she would not quit until God told her to stop. This attitude would resurface in later years when the Wesley brothers allowed women to testify and exhort in their revival meetings.

Both young men were intelligent, and seventeen-year-old John entered Oxford University on a scholarship. He began to read classic devotional books, including *The Imitation of Christ* by Thomas à Kempis. Charles also entered Oxford and started a small group to improve the religious life of its members. They read the remnants of the early desert Christians and adopted a disciplined, methodical approach to their faith. Fellow students coined derisive nicknames for them such as The Holy Club, Bible Moths, and the name that stuck – "Methodists."

With both brothers finished at Oxford, they sailed as missionaries to the new British colony of Georgia in 1735. During the long voyage the ship encountered a huge storm in mid-Atlantic. The main mast broke, and the English settlers on board were screaming in terror. But a group of Moravians, with no fear of dying, calmly sang hymns and prayed. They were followers of Count Nicolas von Zinzendorf. Although the group originated in Moravia, the count recently had welcomed them to his estates in Germany. The Wesleys were impressed at such faith, fearing that theirs fell short of it.

John was to be a pastor in Savannah, the city founded by the colony's governor, General James Oglethorpe, while Charles would be the governor's secretary. But Georgia was hot and humid, crude and dangerous compared to Oxford, and in less than six months Charles sailed home. John managed to stick it out for almost two years before he also returned to England. During his stay in Georgia, he fell in love with a young parishioner, Sophie Hopkey, and he fell hard. When he delayed in pursuing the relationship she eloped with another man, and after much turmoil John left. So, by 1738 the Wesley brothers were back in England feeling like failures as missionaries, as priests, and as Christians.

Remembering the strong faith of the Moravians, John and Charles contacted them in London and began to work with them. In one of their meetings, on May 21, 1738, Charles found himself at peace with God in a way he had never known before. Three nights later John went ("very unwillingly," he wrote) to their meeting on Aldersgate Street. There he heard someone reading from a preface Martin Luther wrote to the book of Romans. John felt his heart "strangely warmed" as he realized in a new way the meaning of Christ's death for him. "I felt I did trust in Christ, Christ alone for salvation; and an assurance was given me that He had taken away my sins, even mine, and saved me from the law of sin and death." That note of assurance captured the hearts of both brothers. Although faithful Anglicans and ordained priests of the church, their faith had been one of striving to obey commandments, do God's will, and live holy lives. Now they knew that no amount of striving could ever win pardon from God, but God had freely offered it in all that Christ was and did. They were saved by grace through faith to do good works.

And the good works followed. With the enthusiasm of new converts, they began to travel and preach for revival in the Church of England. It was the Age of Reason, and churches could be cold, rationalistic, and spiritually dead. The Wesleys brought a note of enthusiasm and emotion that was not always welcome. In order to avoid competing with established worship services, they held their revival meetings at other times. They also adopted a new strategy pioneered by another revival preacher, George Whitefield – they preached outdoors. That brought them into contact with the unchurched population, but in the minds of many this was not the way to do things decently and in order! Courageously they endured opponents who heckled, pelted them with garbage, and even rode horses through the audience. As their movement increased they allowed women to testify and deputized lay assistants to preach. Ever methodical, they organized their followers into small groups for support and accountability but insisted that they remain in the established Church of England. They wanted renewal and revival, not division.

In the course of their work Charles wrote poems, many of which became the contemporary praise and worship music of the day. Writing poetry seemed as natural for him as breathing, and some experts consider Charles Wesley the finest hymn writer in the English language. Among his best known are "O for a Thousand Tongues to Sing," written for the first anniversary of his conversion, "A Charge to Keep I Have," "And Can It Be that I Should Gain?" "Christ the Lord is Risen Today," "Hark! The Herald Angels Sing," "Jesus, Lover of My Soul," "Rejoice, the Lord is King," "Soldiers of Christ, Arise," and "Ye Servants of God, Your Master Proclaim."

While traveling when he was forty, Charles met twenty-year-old Sarah (Sally) Gwinne, a talented musician who sometimes led the singing in their meetings. They married in 1747 and enjoyed a happy life together. Charles made his last nationwide preaching tour in 1756, after which he and Sally settled in Bristol before moving later to London. Several of their children inherited their mother's ability and became noted musicians. Two generations later their grandson Samuel Sebastian Wesley was considered the finest church organist in England.

Meanwhile older brother John also married, in 1751. Because his wife, Mary (Molly) Vazeille, was a wealthy widow, they drew up a prenuptial agreement. John was not to borrow her funds for his ministry, and she would not be responsible for his debts. Their marriage, however, proved to be disastrous. John wanted to follow his calling as a traveling evangelist, but Molly could not understand this. She wanted him to stay at home. Their arguments were vociferous, and she left John several times. At last, he made the following entry in his diary (in Latin): "I did not desert her; I did not send her away; I will not ask her to return." Molly died in 1781, thirty years after they married and ten years after she left for the last time.

John continued crisscrossing England to preach. He also visited Ireland more than once and engaged in active social ministry. He founded an orphanage as well as a school for the children of miners.

In his eighties he went door-to-door in the winter, asking for old clothes he could give to the poor. For his converts and their small group meetings he wrote all kinds of material: Bible studies, commentaries, sermons, condensed classics, tracts, medical advice, and almanacs. He was very learned and could quote the Greek New Testament more easily than its English translations. His own writing was clear and direct, intended to build up his readers rather than his reputation.

When the thirteen colonies in North America declared their independence from British rule in 1776, the Wesleys were horrified. There were almost five thousand "Methodists" in the colonies, but the brothers made no secret of their opposition to revolution against what they saw as lawful authority.

About this time John published *A Collection of Hymns for the Use of … Methodists*. Since many hymns can be sung to more than one tune, the book – true to the practice of that day – contained only the words set out as the poems they really were. Hymnbooks with printed music would come a hundred years later.

As the Methodist movement continued to grow, and for the oversight of those in the new American nation, John Wesley made a fateful decision in 1784. Claiming he had the authority to ordain "superintendents" for the American work, he sent Francis Asbury and Thomas Coke to the United States. This had the effect of doing what he never intended to do – start a new denomination. "Methodist," originally used as an insult, then the name of a movement, was now the title of an organization.

Charles Wesley died on March 28, 1788, at the age of eighty-one. John outlived his younger brother, dying on May 2, 1791, at the age of eighty-seven. Just one month before his death he was busy planning another preaching tour through England. Today Wesley's Chapel, surrounded by London's urban sprawl, continues to be an active congregation. Next door stands the house where the small, energetic man spent his final years. In Bristol, Charles and Sally's early home, there is another chapel where the brothers met and trained the preachers of their movement. Two striking statues grace the chapel grounds.

Charles stands with arms outstretched in a welcoming pastoral gesture while John is in the saddle, eager to ride on to the next evangelistic opportunity.

Together they lived and died as faithful ministers in the Church of England. Together they ignited a movement that today is the largest Protestant denomination in the northern United States, with missions and outreach around the globe. Together they created a body of writing, both poetry and prose, still useful more than two hundred years later. They embodied an attitude reflected in a statement John once made: "Is thy heart with my heart? Then give me thy hand!"

In the Voice of the Wesleys

No one knows exactly how many poems Charles Wesley composed. John wrote some too, and they published them together without names on them. Today those closest to the work of Charles estimate his output at about nine thousand pieces of verse. As Thomas à Kempis and John Bunyan laced their prose with biblical echoes, so Charles Wesley did with his poetry. "Love Divine," written in the year of his marriage, is one of his most famous. It deserves careful study, among other reasons for its many biblical allusions.

Love Divine

1. Love divine, all loves excelling,
Joy of heaven, to earth come down;
Fix in us thy humble dwelling;
All thy faithful mercies crown!
Jesus, thou art all compassion,
Pure, unbounded love thou art;
Visit us with thy salvation;
Enter every trembling heart.

2. Breathe, O breathe thy loving Spirit
Into every troubled breast!
Let us all in thee inherit;
Let us find that second rest.
Take away our bent to sinning;
Alpha and Omega be;
End of faith, as its beginning,
Set our hearts at liberty.

3. Come, Almighty, to deliver,
Let us all thy life receive;
Suddenly return and never,
Never-more thy temples leave.
Thee we would be always blessing,
Serve thee as thy hosts above,
Pray and praise thee without ceasing,
Glory in thy perfect love.

4. Finish, then, thy new creation;
Pure and spotless let us be.
Let us see thy great salvation
Perfectly restored in thee;
Changed from glory into glory,
Till in heaven we take our place,
Till we cast our crowns before thee,
Lost in wonder, love, and praise.

In 1755 John Wesley inaugurated a Covenant Service in which Methodists were urged to renew their commitment to God. He issued a pamphlet containing the order for the service which has been modified through the years. Its climax is the covenant prayer spoken by the minister and the people together.

A Covenant Prayer

I am no longer my own, but thine.
Put me to what thou wilt, rank me with whom thou wilt:
Put me to doing, put me to suffering:
Let me be employed for thee, or laid aside for thee:
Exalted for thee, or brought low for thee:
Let me be full, let me be empty:
Let me have all things, let me have nothing:
I freely and heartily yield all things to thy pleasure and disposal.
And now, O glorious and blessed God,
    Father, Son and Holy Spirit,
Thou art mine and I am thine. So be it.
And the covenant which I have made on earth,
    let it be ratified in heaven. Amen
"John Wesley's Covenant Service" (Nashville: Discipleship Resources, n.d.), p. 6.

The spiritual influence of John and Charles Wesley resulted in a world-wide revival and the advent of a new denomination. Our next friend had less institutional impact, but his writings, especially those collected by his wife in *My Upmost for His Highest*, have surely had a daily influence on millions of believers.

13

IRREVERENT REVEREND

OSWALD CHAMBERS

A visitor who encountered Oswald Chambers for the first time described him as "the most irreverent Reverend I ever met." Apparently the clergyman's rollicking sense of humor was too much for them. But there was more to Oswald Chambers than laughter – there was deep, grateful love for God and passion to share it with others. Until his tragic early death, he wanted only to give, as he put it, "my utmost for His highest." That phrase became the title of what may be the world's most widely used book of daily devotions. If so, he must be a classic friend.

Oswald Chambers was a Scotsman, born in 1874, the seventh of eight children. His father was a Baptist pastor, and Oswald grew up in Perth where he and his brothers relished everything out of doors. Their father moved the family to London in 1889, and the next year went to hear the great Charles Spurgeon preach. He was so moved that he came home and urged his sixteen-year-old son to believe in Christ for salvation and be baptized, which he did.

Oswald Chambers was artistically gifted, so he attended the National Art Training School which awarded him a Master's Certificate in 1895. He went on to the University of Edinburgh where he received a degree in art. But he was wrestling with a call to Christian ministry, and the next four years were, as he put it, "hell on earth." Bypassing seminaries and university faculties of divinity, he enrolled in a small Scottish

Bible school. There he experienced a crisis of faith in November 1901. "Either Christianity is a downright fraud," he exclaimed, "or I have not got hold of the right end of the stick." By faith he believed Jesus' promise of the Holy Spirit for those who ask, and his life took on new power and joy.

He taught for a year at a Bible school in Cincinnati and then in Japan before returning to England where he became active in meetings for holiness and revival. On one of his transatlantic voyages, he met Gertrude Hobbs (he called her Biddy), and a warm friendship developed between them. Courtship followed, which led to their marriage in 1910. The next year they founded the Bible Training College in London to prepare candidates for missionary service, and three years later their daughter Kathleen was born. Biddy was an expert in high-speed shorthand (her dream was to become secretary to the prime minister). She took notes on Oswald's chapel talks to the students and filed them away. It wasn't all work, though, not when Oswald Chambers was around. He sometimes dismissed classes for a day and took the tiny student body into the countryside for a picnic – so he could spend the afternoon fishing!

With the outbreak of World War I, the couple closed the missionary training school in order to become missionaries themselves. Under the auspices of the Young Men's Christian Association, they began to work among the British troops stationed in Zeitoun, Egypt. The army camp was located outside Cairo near the famous pyramids of Giza. There Oswald manned the YMCA hut – a tent, really – twelve hours a day, gave nightly Bible talks which Biddy faithfully recorded, led discussions, and counseled troubled soldiers. Among her other activities, Biddy hosted Sunday afternoon teas complete with tablecloths, fresh flowers, and mounds of cake. More than four hundred lonely British soldiers responded to her hospitality.

By mid-1917, extreme heat, overwork, and fatigue had worn down Oswald's physical resistance. His gaunt body developed appendicitis. Although he underwent surgery, he died shortly afterward on November 15 from complications of the infection. He was forty-three years old. Biddy wanted only a small, private funeral for her husband, but the troops would not agree. Chambers was buried at Zeitoun with full military honors. Uniformed officers pulled the gun carriage bearing his coffin, and one hundred volunteers accompanied it to the cemetery. There they laid him to rest among the men he had served.

Widowed at thirty-four, Biddy continued her work among the troops and also began to print some of Oswald's sermons for distribution. After the war ended she and Kathleen returned to England where they eked out a living as best they could. In the years that followed, Biddy transcribed her shorthand notes and assembled a collection of them in a devotional book which she called *My Utmost for His Highest* (1927). Each dated page contained a short scripture passage followed by Oswald's explanation and application, never more than five hundred words. His message to missionary and military recruits began to catch the attention of Christians everywhere. Sounding at times like a biblical prophet confronting indifferent Israel, or Thomas à Kempis addressing novice monks, Chambers encouraged and exhorted, probed and provoked, all to get the best that believers could give to God. The book spawned an industry which continues to this day in a variety of electronic and print formats.

Working at home, Biddy prepared several dozen other books from her shorthand notes and dealt with as many as fifty letters a day responding to her husband's message. One letter which found its way to her was addressed simply "Mrs. Oswald Chambers, London." With the onset of World War II, demand for Chambers' books increased, but then tragedy struck. German firebombs hit the London warehouse where the books were stored, destroying all forty thousand copies. But the demand continued, and the supply was recreated. Biddy selflessly continued her work of publishing her husband's words, always maintaining an open house for visitors and missionaries, until she died in 1966. Kathleen, a nurse, shared the house with her mother and more visitors until she died in 1997 at the age of eighty-three. Before her death she was able to furnish valuable information to David

McCasland for his biography *Oswald Chambers: Abandoned to God* (1992), and he dedicated the book to her.

In Chambers' Voice

My Utmost for His Highest, unlike the books already described, is not a piece of sustained writing. Its single-page units address a different topic each day, although several days may be connected. Therefore, we must treat it in a different way, and we will leave the punctuation marks and capital letters where Biddy placed them when she published it in 1927.

As her transcriptions show, Oswald Chambers was passionate about what God has given us in Christ and what we need to give in return. If God so loved the world that he gave his one and only Son, then we must respond with our "utmost" to this gift of "His highest." For Chambers, this is more than a mountaintop experience or a momentary emotion – it means obedience, obedience in the details of life over the long haul.

For the Long Haul One of the great snares of Christian workers is to make a fetish of our rare moments. . . . If you make a god out of your best moments," he counseled, "God will fade out of your life and never come back until you do the duty that lies nearest. . . . (April 25). Beware of a surrender which you make to God in an ecstasy; you are apt to take it back again. It is a question of being united with Jesus in His death until nothing ever appeals to you that did not appeal to Him (September 13).

Obedience Obedience as Chambers described it means surrendering our will to God as disclosed in Jesus Christ. He is the final word on reality, the ultimate sacrifice for our sinfulness. Chambers wrote that "the pietistic movements of today have none of the rugged reality of the New Testament about them; there is nothing about them that needs the Death of Jesus Christ; all that is required is a pious atmosphere and prayer and devotion. . . . The type of Christian experience in the New Testament is that of personal passionate devotion to the Person of Jesus Christ. Every other type of Christian experience, so called, is detached from the Person of Jesus Christ. . . . In the New Testament Jesus Christ is Saviour long before He is Pattern. Today He is being dispatched as the Figurehead of a Religion, a mere Example. He is that, but He is infinitely more. He is salvation itself. He *is* the Gospel of God. . . . When I commit myself to the revelation made in the New Testament, I receive from God the Gift of the Holy Spirit Who begins to interpret to me what Jesus did; and does in me subjectively all that Jesus Christ did for me objectively" (November 29).

Our Response On our part, this calls for a response of radical faith and willed obedience as empowered by the Spirit of Jesus. "Decide for Christ is an emphasis on something Our Lord never trusted. He never asks us to decide for Him, but to yield to Him – a very different thing" (August 21). "The tiniest detail in which I obey has all the omnipotent power of the grace of God behind it" (June 15). This, wrote Chambers, is the way to deal with uncertainty and confusion in our lives. The key lies not in consultation, consecration, or even prayer. It is found in obedience. "You cannot think a spiritual muddle clear, you have to obey it clear . . . and all the thinking we like to spend on it will never make it clear. Spiritual muddle is only made plain by obedience. Immediately we obey, we discern" (September 14).

Prayer. Chambers, like so many before and after him, insists that prayer should move beyond claiming God's gifts to knowing God as Giver. "Whenever the insistence is on the point that God answers prayer, we are off the track. The meaning of prayer is that we get hold of God, not of the answer" (February 7). "Prayer is not simply getting things from God . . ; prayer is getting into perfect communion with God" (September 16). This may mean dark times when God no longer seems to be speaking to us. What then? How do we respond when there is no word from the Lord, only silence – no light on the mountain, only darkness? "God's silences are His answers. . . . His silence is the sign that He is bringing you into a marvelous understanding of Himself. . . . He will give you the first sign of His intimacy – silence" (October 11).

Suffering. Another sign of intimacy may be suffering, and Chambers refused to shy away from it. We must embrace it as part of our service to God in the world. "God breaks up the private life of His saints, and makes it a thoroughfare for the world on the one hand and for Himself on the other. No human beings can stand that unless they are identified with Jesus Christ" (November 1). "We make calls out of our own spiritual consecration, but when we get right with God He brushes all these aside, and rivets us with a pain that is terrific to one thing we never dreamed of. . . . This call has nothing to do with personal sanctification, but with being made broken bread and poured-out wine. God can never make us wine if we object to the fingers He uses to crush us with" (September 30). "God plants His saints in the most useless places. We say – God intends me to be here because I am so useful. Jesus never estimated His life along the lines of the greatest use. God puts His saints where they will glorify Him, and we are no judges at all of where that is" (August 10). What God desires more than our service is our very selves. "As long as you have the tiniest bit of spiritual impertinence, it will always reveal itself in the fact that you are expecting God to tell you to do a big thing, and all He is telling you to do is to 'come'" (October 8). "No Christian has a special work to do. . . . Our Lord calls to no special work: He calls to Himself" (October 16).

Life. As Chambers sees it, all of this impacts all of life. "When we do anything from a sense of duty, we can back it up by argument; when we do anything in obedience to the Lord, there is no argument possible; that is why a saint can be easily ridiculed" (February 28). "... [T]he message must be part of ourselves. The Son of God was His own message . . . ; and as His disciples our lives must be the sacrament of our message" (March 10). "The new life manifests itself in conscious repentance and unconscious holiness" (August 15). "Certainty is the mark of the common-sense life; gracious uncertainty is the mark of the spiritual life" (April 29). "Watch the things you shrug your shoulders over, and you will know why you do not go on spiritually" (July 27). "Unless in the first waking moment of the day you learn to fling the door wide back and let God in, you will work on a wrong level all day; but swing the door wide open and pray to your Father in secret, and every public thing will be stamped with the presence of God" (August 23).

Like the humorous Chambers, our next spiritual guide may not have appeared to be a deep spiritual person from a surface view. Yet the witty Evelyn Underhill was one whose friendship with those of us she would never meet continues to lead many to the heart of God, even today.

14

NOT BROUGHT UP TO RELIGION

EVELYN UNDERHILL

Charles Williams told of a time when he was with Evelyn Underhill and she appeared to glow with light. Pleasant, friendly, and witty, she was not what people expected in a world-famous spiritual writer. She enjoyed travel, cats, and bridge as well as books, Bibles, and cathedrals. In fact, it was travel to Europe's churches and art galleries that first piqued this English girl's interest in matters of the spirit.

She was born in 1875, the only child of a well-to-do British lawyer and his wife. The family's comfortable position enabled them to take extensive vacations of yachting and travel. But, as Evelyn wrote years later, "I wasn't brought up to religion." All the same, the beauty of sea and mountains, together with the awe she felt in cathedrals and before great art, touched the young girl. From early life she was interested in the spiritual. At first it was a general intrigue with the magic of what makes good things happen. For several years she belonged to what some have called an occult society. The members and the meetings were devoted to the study of ritual magic to align with the positive forces in the world.

Extremely intelligent, Evelyn attended and graduated from King's College for Women in London. She discovered she had gifts as a writer and poet and began to publish under the name John Cordelier. Perhaps a male identity would make her work more acceptable. At the same time, she was becoming disenchanted with trying to manipulate the forces of the universe. She turned her attention toward the church, the Roman Catholic Church of soaring cathedrals and great art. It was a time, however, when the hierarchy was cracking down on intellectuals who might challenge its beliefs and traditions – and Miss Underhill was an independent intellectual. Besides, her fiancé, longtime friend Hubert Stuart Moore, opposed the idea of her going to a priest for confession. He wanted no one standing between him and his wife-to-be. So Evelyn settled for life as a nominal member of the Church of England, and in 1907 she and Hubert were married.

The marriage was a happy one although not blessed with children. Hubert, like her father, was an attorney and became a respected expert in maritime law. Also like her father, he had little interest in religion but allowed Evelyn to pursue hers. Both enjoyed their respective occupations as well as evenings together at home when not attending some social function. Their life was a comfortable one, aided by domestic help who cared for all mundane matters. Thus Mrs. Stuart Moore, as she was formally known, was free to study, ponder, and write as much as she wished. In her thirties and disenchanted with magic, she began to research the subject of mysticism, especially in light of the new study of psychology. Were claims of mystical experience legitimate? How could they be explained? And what of the older disciplines of philosophy and theology?

In 1911 she published the results of her research in *Mysticism: A Study of the Nature and Development of Spiritual Consciousness*. It was her first book under her own name, and the most famous. Part One, "The Mystic Fact," examined the phenomenon of mysticism in light of the disciplines mentioned above. Part Two, "The Mystic Way," described the path most mystics have walked from awakening and purification through the dark night of the soul to life in union with God. A densely packed appendix traced the history of mysticism in Europe up to the death of William Blake in 1827. In its final twelfth edition (1931), the five-hundred-page volume concluded with a bibliography of thirty pages and a complete index.

Instantly, Evelyn Underhill was on the minds of those who studied and thought about these things. She attracted the special attention of Friedrich von Hugel, who was emerging as the finest Catholic theologian in England. For almost fifteen years, Underhill and von Hugel were in contact through correspondence and personal visits. Old enough to be her father, he was a hereditary Baron of the Holy Roman Empire, a progressive but devout Catholic, a family man with a wife and three daughters (one of whom became a nun), an independent philosopher of religion, a genius fluent in a handful of languages, and a man of deep sensitivity and suffering.

Von Hugel wrote to Underhill after he read *Mysticism*, noting what he believed to be its strengths and weaknesses. As a progressive Catholic he was in contact with various liberal scholars, placing him in danger of discipline or even excommunication. Underhill, meanwhile, was a nominal Anglican who felt that much Christian practice was sentimental and too focused on Jesus. For the next ten years she continued to write about mysticism, pouring out a stream of reviews, articles, and books. But she sensed that something was missing in her life, so in 1921 she approached the Baron (as she called him) with a proposal: would he become her spiritual director? The idea was not unheard of, but the specifics were unusual. Spiritual direction was usually given by ordained priests to other clergy, to monks or nuns, and perhaps to interested laypersons. But von Hugel was neither professor nor priest – he was a layman. Further, he was nearly deaf from an illness in his teenage years. Anyone wishing to speak with him would need to shout or at least speak very distinctly. And he was quite patriarchal, insisting that Evelyn always sit on a low footstool at his feet (or did he believe that might help his hearing?).

From 1921 until his death in 1925, Evelyn Underhill placed herself under von Hugel's guidance. Sometimes they could talk face-to-face, but much of his direction to her came in correspondence. Always he was deliberate, thoughtful, and sensitive. He quickly sized up her religion as out of balance, too cerebral. "You have too much blood going to your brain," he said, so he asked her to spend two afternoons each week visiting the poor. However difficult this may have been at first for the refined Mrs. Moore, she continued the practice until ill health later forced her to stop. She came to feel special affection for a particular single mother trying to raise several children. The welfare mom and the famous writer became close friends. One of Underhill's best books, *The House of the Soul* (1929), bears a dedication to that mother: "For Rosa, with my love." The Baron's direction had produced a revolution in the life of his directee.

A second revolution also occurred, as Evelyn herself described in a letter she wrote in 1926. "Until about five years ago [when she began spiritual direction with von Hugel] I had never had any personal experience of our Lord: I didn't know what it meant. I was a convinced theocentric, thought most Christocentric language and practice sentimental and superstitious and was very handy with shallow psychological explanations of it. I had from time to time what seemed to be vivid experiences of God, from the time of my conversion from agnosticism (about twenty years ago now). This position I thought to be that of a broad-minded and intelligent Christian, but when, after a severe spiritual smash and partial recovery, I went to the Baron, he said I wasn't much better than a Unitarian! Somehow by his prayers or something he *compelled* me to experience Christ. He never said anything more about it — but I know humanly speaking he did it. It took about four months — it was like watching the sun rise very slowly — and then suddenly one knew what it was" [letter to Bishop Walter Howard Frere, quoted in *Fragments from an Inner Life*, ed. by Dana Greene (Harrisburg, PA: Morehouse Publishing, 1993), p. 78f.].

The result of all this was a subtle shift in her writing. From the Baron's death in 1925 until her own in 1941, Underhill's output became more Christ-centered, as classical doctrines such as incarnation and atonement, the church and the sacraments were evident. Also clear was the need to be faithful in all of life, whether it be work or worship.

Evelyn Underhill lived sixteen years beyond her beloved Baron. Life without him was hard, but hers took a new direction. Although she had been the first woman ever invited to lecture on religion at

Oxford University (1921), academia was not her calling. Instead, she found herself becoming a sought-after speaker for spiritual retreats. Beginning with *The House of the Soul*, she wrote and published numerous small books of the talks she gave at retreats. But asthma gripped her more and more, and her health grew increasingly fragile. She wrote one set of talks each year, refined them in the retreats where she spoke, and then they were ready to publish. For many people, these small books are the reason why they love and respect this woman who eventually was called the spiritual director for a whole generation of Anglicans.

At sixty years of age, she completed the other major research project of her life, a book titled simply *Worship*. In it she explored what worship is as our creaturely response to our creator. She addressed the character and principles of worship, both corporate and personal. And she described worship as it occurs in various traditions, both Jewish and Christian. This work, together with *Mysticism*, created virtual bookends for her writing career with her briefer books coming in between. She learned in 1938 that Scotland's University of Aberdeen intended to award her an honorary Doctor of Divinity degree. Husband Hubert was excited and she was pleased, but failing health prevented her from traveling to accept the honor even when the university postponed it for a year.

Not long after *Worship* was released, World War II broke out in Europe. In World War I, Evelyn had worked as a translator and writer for British naval intelligence, but now her mind had changed. She had come to believe that Jesus' teachings and example called Christians to pacifism, and she wrote to say so. It was the first time she publicly aligned herself with a political position. She was thrilled at the evacuation of British troops from Dunkirk in 1940 – C. S. Lewis's brother among them – but alarmed at the use of religion to support the war. As German bombs rained down on London night after night, she and Hubert were forced to leave their large, comfortable house. Their neighborhood had been hit, and friends outside the city gave them refuge. Bronchitis only worsened her asthma, and she required morphine for intense pain. The end came on June 15, 1941, when she died at the age of sixty-five. Her will contained one final expression of her faith. It directed that her funeral should be a celebration of life with no mourning, no flowers, and no "lugubrious hymns"!

Evelyn Underhill's reputation has continued in the decades following her death. Almost all her thirty-nine books are still in print – an amazing feat. Those published after her direction from von Hugel (1921-25) are usually considered more dependable, but the earlier ones also contain much insight and wisdom. *Mysticism* and *Worship* remain standard works in their fields, still used today as upper-level textbooks. Twelve of her retreats from 1924-36 have been published, but a thirteenth sadly is lost. Among those considered her best are *Abba*, *The Golden Sequence*, and *The House of the Soul*. Another set of talks, *Concerning the Inner Life*, was given in 1926 to Anglican clergy, the first by a layperson, especially a woman. She continues to be the object of research and writing, a favorite of scholars both female and male. In 1988 the Episcopal Church of America added her name to those honored in its calendar of the church year, describing her as a theologian and mystic.

In Underhill's Voice

Along with her books, in her lifetime Evelyn Underhill wrote hundreds of articles and reviews. After her death her letters were published with a brilliant introduction by Charles Williams, a friend of Evelyn and of C. S. Lewis. Here is some wisdom from *Concerning the Inner Life*, her 1926 retreat talks to Anglican clergy.

Union With God. . . . St. Theresa [of Avila] says that if anyone claiming to be united to God is always in a state of peaceful beatitude, she simply does not believe in their union with God. Such a union, to her mind, involves great sorrow for the sin and pain of the world; a sense of identity not only with God but also with all other souls, and a great longing to redeem and heal. That is real supernatural charity. It is a call to love and save not the nice but the nasty; not the lovable but the unlovely, the hard, the narrow, and the embittered, and the tiresome, who are so much worse. . . . [T]his will only be done by maintaining and feeding the temper of adoration and trustful adherence. This is the heart of the life of prayer; and only in so far as we work from this center can we safely dare to touch other souls and seek to affect them [*The House of the Soul* and *Concerning the Inner Life* (Minneapolis: Seabury Press, n.d.), p. 140f.].

Spiritual Life *The Spiritual Life* (1937) is a series of four talks Evelyn Underhill gave on the radio in 1936. It may be the simplest of all her books, directed as it was to a very general and diverse audience.

When . . . we lift our eyes from the crowded by-pass to the eternal hills, then how much the personal and practical things we have to deal with are enriched. What meaning and coherence come into our scattered lives. We mostly spend those lives conjugating three verbs: to Want, to Have, and to Do. Craving, clutching, and fussing, on the material, political, social, emotional, intellectual – even on the religious – plane, we are kept in perpetual unrest: forgetting that none of these verbs have any ultimate significance, except so far as they are transcended by and included in, the fundamental verb, to Be: and that Being, not wanting, having and doing, is the essence of a spiritual life ["What Is the Spiritual Life?" in *The Spiritual Life* (London: Hodder and Stoughton, 1937), p. 19f.].

God seems to be no respecter of our ecclesiastical traditions. Evelyn Underhill, largely self-educated in her field and a highly liturgical Anglican, is a classic friend. Another is the almost over-educated, non-liturgical Quaker, Thomas Raymond Kelly.

15

PURSUING ADEQUACY

THOMAS R. KELLY

On January 17, 1941, a college professor in suburban Philadelphia announced to his wife, "Today will be the greatest day of my life." Thomas Kelly had just written to the religion editor of Harper and Brothers, accepting an invitation to speak with him about producing a little book on devotional practice. Kelly was becoming known for the freshness, power, and authenticity of his writing. But that evening, while drying the dinner dishes, he slumped to the floor in cardiac arrest. His wife and children could only watch helplessly as he moaned softly and died.

Dr. Kelly was forty-seven years old, a professor of philosophy at Haverford College, the elite among Quaker schools in America. His colleague and friend Douglas Steere wrote of him, "The story of Thomas Kelly's life is the story of a passionate and determined quest for adequacy" (*A Testament of Devotion,* 1996, p. 103). For three years he had been teaching, preaching, and writing from a spiritual reality few people could fathom. For two decades prior to that he had experienced drivenness, distraction, and depression, but no longer. Now he was – to everyone's amazement – integrated and whole, simplified, loving, and joyful. His church trusted him with leadership, colleagues respected him with awe, and his two young children adored him.

Kelly's journey began in southern Ohio where he was born in 1893 into a devout Quaker family. Ohio Quakers had been touched by the nineteenth century's revival movements and did not always maintain traditional Quaker ways. Young Tom was just four when his father died. His mother wanted her children to receive a good education, so she moved the family to Wilmington, Ohio, where Quakers had started a small college. There Kelly majored in chemistry, delighted to discover the world of hard facts and scientific knowledge. He also indulged his penchant for pranks, such as riding his motorcycle across the campus at breakneck speed. After graduation he went to Haverford College for further study in chemistry, and on his first day met the famed philosopher Rufus Jones. In his excitement he said to Dr. Jones, "I am just going to make my life a miracle!"

That enthusiasm carried him the next year to Canada where he taught science, but a drive for more learning drew him back to the States. World War I intervened, and in the best Quaker fashion he volunteered to serve wherever needed. He spent nearly a year working in England with German prisoners, the beginning of what became a longstanding concern for the people of Germany. Back home he entered Hartford Theological Seminary, graduating in 1919. The next day he married his fiancée Lael Macy, and then returned to Wilmington College as professor of Bible. Two years of that and his restlessness drove him back to Hartford to begin Ph.D. studies in philosophy, which he completed in 1924. He not only received his degree but also was elected to the prestigious honors society Phi Beta Kappa.

Quaker leaders in America then asked Dr. and Mrs. Kelly to go to Europe and work with their relief centers in Berlin and Vienna. The goal was to lead them in becoming hubs of Quaker study and service for all who might be interested. Thomas Kelly's intellectual ability, familiarity with Quaker life, deep spirituality, and his fluency in the German language combined to make him the ideal choice for the delicate job. The Kellys returned from Germany in 1925, locating in Richmond, Indiana, where Tom began to teach philosophy at Earlham College. He was thirty-two, convinced that hard-nosed academic life was his true calling. His earlier joy with chemistry now echoed in the all-out passion with which he approached philosophy. Despite that,

117

students found him interesting, approachable, and full of much good humor. After five years Kelly moved his wife and their two-year-old daughter to Massachusetts in further pursuit of his passion for academic achievement.

He wanted most of all to become a world-class scholar, which in his mind meant a Ph.D. in philosophy from Harvard University. He already possessed the degree from Hartford with Phi Beta Kappa honors, but that was not enough. With little precedent for anyone seeking a second doctorate in the same field, Harvard reluctantly admitted him to begin research which he finally completed in 1937. It would have to be piecemeal, for along the way he taught at Wellesley College in Massachusetts, again in Indiana at Earlham, and then at the University of Hawaii. At the latter school he was able to interact with Asian scholars and study Eastern philosophies in his quest for world-class knowledge. A son was born into the family there, so the Kellys were now a family of four. But funds were scarce and borrowed, and Tom's health was often threatened. He experienced severe hay fever, kidney stone attacks, sinus infection requiring surgery, and "nervous exhaustion," all of which rendered him bedfast at times.

Fortune smiled at last in 1936 when Haverford College invited him to join their faculty. His colleague in philosophy would be Douglas Steere, eventually perhaps the century's most famous American Quaker. Kelly moved quickly to complete the work for his Harvard doctorate, wrote his dissertation, and it was published to good reviews. In the autumn of 1937, he traveled to Massachusetts for the final step – the oral defense of his new dissertation. There he lived out the nightmare of every doctoral candidate. In the stress of the examination his mind went blank. He could remember nothing of what he had studied, learned, or written. This had happened years before when he finished his first Ph.D. Back then the Hartford examiners had sympathized, encouraged him, and he recovered to give a brilliant defense of his research. But the Harvard committee was not so kind. They failed him on the examination and told him he could never have a second chance. He returned to Philadelphia defeated, despondent, and – his wife feared – suicidal. He had failed himself, his family, and his calling. It had all been for nothing – all the moves, all the family disruption, the years of study, sacrifice, indebtedness, and broken health – it was for nothing.

When her husband arrived home that evening, Lael Kelly quickly called for Douglas Steere and the college president to come to the house. They reminded Tom that he already had a Ph.D. in philosophy, assured him that his job was not in jeopardy, and promised there would be no announcement of what had happened. In the weeks that followed Steere walked with Kelly through his dark night of grief. More than anyone except Lael Kelly, Douglas Steere knew Thomas Kelly's despair. Then, as Steere described it, "No one knows exactly what happened, but a strained period in his life was over. He moved toward adequacy. A fissure in him seemed to close, cliffs caved in and filled up a chasm, and what was divided grew together within him." He spoke and wrote with "the same voice, the same pen, the same rich imagery that always crowded his writing, and on the whole a remarkably similar set of religious ideas. But now he seemed to be expounding less as one possessed of '*knowledge about*' and more as one who had had unmistakable '*acquaintance with*'" (*A Testament of Devotion*, 1996, p. 118f.).

As Kelly resumed his usual life word spread about the authenticity, freshness, and power of what he had to say. Quaker groups invited him to speak, and their magazines welcomed his essays and articles. The American Friends Service Committee asked him to go once more to Germany in the summer of 1938, for it seemed clear the Nazi government would soon seal the borders. Away from his family, he traveled for weeks visiting Quaker groups, speaking when asked, listening and encouraging as much as possible. Deeply moved by the injustice and suffering he saw, he knelt to pray in the great cathedral at Cologne. There he felt God laid the burden of the entire world on him, then assured him that with divine help it could be borne. Kelly would later say that God doesn't want us to carry the whole world, but only what has been personally given to us. As he put it, "We cannot die on *every* cross, nor are we expected to" (*A Testament of Devotion*, 1996, p. 83).

He returned from Germany in September, the last passenger to leave the steamship. In the weeks that followed he often said to his friends, "I have been literally melted down by the love of God." He wrote to Rufus Jones, now his mentor, "I have longed to talk about *Him* who deals so tenderly and lovingly to undeserving hearts" (*A Testament of Devotion,* 1996, p. 121). That sense of human undeserving, divine grace, and the spontaneous response of grateful love marked his life for the next three years. He had found the adequacy for which he sought so long, but it was a divine gift rather than the fruit of his quest. Around him gathered a small group of college students who met with him to read spiritual classics, discuss their meaning, and prepare to move out into lives of worshipful service. Dr. Kelly himself lived more fully than ever, relishing family and friends. Vacations in Maine, building toys for his children, and his boyish humor were special delights. He continued to teach, speak, and write for Quakers beyond Philadelphia until the evening of his fatal heart attack, and then suddenly it was over.

When Kelly died, his colleague Douglas Steere was on sabbatical leave. He cut it in half in order to substitute in his friend's classes and sift through the essays, articles, and lectures Kelly had left behind. From them he selected five, added a biographical memoir, and titled the collection *A Testament of Devotion.* It was a testament to God's amazing grace, Kelly's devotion to God, and his calling as a committed follower of Christ. In some ways his message resembled Brother Lawrence's moment-by-moment practice of the presence of God. As Kelly himself put it, "Continuously renewed immediacy, not receding memory of the Divine Touch, lies at the base of religious living.... Religion as a dull habit is not that for which Christ lived and died" (*A Testament of Devotion,* 1996, pp. 5, 27).

Although Kelly said almost nothing about himself in its pages, the note of personal experience in the book was strong. Readers quickly learned they could find themselves in its one hundred pages. The final essay, "The Simplification of Life," concludes with a reference to death. Otherwise, its contents could have placed it first, to be followed by the other chapters: "The Light Within," "Holy Obedience," "The Blessed Community," and "The Eternal Now and Social Concern." Harper and Brothers, which originally wanted to consider Kelly's work, published the book in 1941 and has never allowed it to go out of print. In 1966, twenty-five years after his death, they released another collection of his material, *The Eternal Hope*, together with *Thomas Kelly: A Biography,* by his son Richard.

In Kelly's Voice

Thomas Kelly's essay "The Simplification of Life" is a favorite of many readers. Written for a symposium on the subject in 1939, it still rings true nearly ninety years later. Although titled to speak of simplifying, the essay speaks powerfully about the *integration* of life. It especially addresses readers who feel driven and pressured, divided and weakened by their many concerns. It offers gentle wisdom about God's healing of our spirits so we become whole, complete, integrated human beings. Here are its concluding paragraphs.

Life from the Center. Much of our acceptance of multitudes of obligations is due to our inability to say No. We calculated that that task had to be done, and we saw no one ready to undertake it. We calculated the need, and then calculated our time, and decided maybe we could squeeze it in somewhere. But the decision was a heady decision, not made within the sanctuary of the soul.

When we say Yes or No to calls for service on the basis of heady decisions, we have to give reasons, to ourselves and to others. But when we say Yes or No to calls for service on the basis of inner guidance and whispered promptings of encouragement from the Center of our life, or on the basis of a lack of any inward 'rising' of that Life to encourage us in the call, we have no reason to give, except one – the will of God as we discern it. Then we have begun to live in guidance.

And I find God never guides us into an intolerable scramble of panting feverishness. The Cosmic Patience becomes, in part, our patience for after all God is at work in the world. It is not we alone who are at work in the world, frantically finishing a work to be offered to God.

Life from the Center is a life of unhurried peace and power. It is simple. It is serene. It is amazing. It is triumphant. It is radiant. It takes no time, but it occupies all our time. And it makes our life programs new and overcoming. We need not get frantic. God is at the helm. And when our little day is done we lie down quietly in peace, for all is well [Thomas R. Kelly, *A Testament of Devotion* (HarperSanFrancisco, 1996), p. 99f.].

When Thomas Kelly visited Germany shortly before World War II, one of the people he met was a young rabbi destined for fame, Abraham Joshua Heschel. Another of the most famous figures to emerge from that terrible time was a young Lutheran whose tragic story has gone around the world. He too is a classic friend.

16

MARTYRED PROPHET

DIETRICH BONHOEFFER

Few children have grown up with such joyful privilege as Dietrich Bonhoeffer, born in Breslau, Germany, in 1906. He and his twin sister Sabine were the sixth and seventh of Dr. Karl and Paula Bonhoeffer's eight children. When Dietrich was six his father, a prominent physician, moved the family to the capital where he became one of Berlin University's first professors of psychiatry. In spite of Germany's role and defeat in World War I – and the death in it of his oldest brother Walter – Dietrich grew up in a warm atmosphere of learning and the arts. He and his siblings often played with the children of other professors, some of them world-famous scholars. It soon became clear that he was gifted intellectually and artistically, especially as a skilled pianist.

To the dismay of his family, he announced in his early teens that he wanted to be a theologian. Dietrich pursued his goal, completing the equivalent of a Ph.D. at the age of twenty-one. He followed that with a year in Barcelona, Spain, where he pastored a German-speaking congregation. Returning home, he wrote a second dissertation, which qualified him to become a university professor. To prepare himself still further, he spent the next year at Union Theological Seminary in New York City. There he appreciated the vibrancy of African American worship in Harlem and the concern of American students for the poor. But he was disappointed with their low interest in theology. Upon his return to Germany the twenty-five-year-old was appointed, like his father, to the faculty of Berlin's prestigious university.

But life in Germany had changed. The nation was in turmoil over their harsh treatment after World War I, the effects of economic depression in the country, and the threat of aggressive Soviet Communism. The Germans elected Adolf Hitler as their *Führer* (leader) in 1933, trusting that he would propel them to national greatness. Only days later Dietrich Bonhoeffer, still in his twenties but with prophetic insight, publicly opposed this in a radio broadcast. He was prepared to say that without proper limits, the new Leader could become the Misleader – a sign of things to come.

Now all professors had to swear an oath of loyalty to the new regime and open their classes with the salute "Heil Hitler!" The state assumed management of the churches, and Nazi flags covered communion tables and altars. Hitler's dream of Aryan supremacy was lifted up while Jews and other minorities were actively hunted and persecuted. National Socialism was identified not only as the historical moment, but as the very will of God. In the opinion of people like the Bonhoeffer family, Hitler's word had become law and the situation was intolerable.

Young Dr. Bonhoeffer responded in several ways. Believing that his career had lost its proper meaning, he abandoned academia. In autumn 1933 he moved to London where he served as pastor of two churches. There he tried to explain the struggle for Germany's soul to British Christians. But, with few exceptions, their leaders and churches were not ready to deal with Hitler and Nazism.

Second, Bonhoeffer identified with the Confessing Church, an ecumenical movement which opposed what Hitler was doing. Representatives from various churches met at Barmen in 1934 and drafted what became known as the Barmen Declaration. It opens with these words: "The impregnable foundation of the German Evangelical [i.e., Protestant] Church is the gospel of Jesus Christ, as it is revealed in Holy Scripture and came again to the light in the creeds of the Reformation. In this way the authorities, which the church needs for her mission, are defined and limited." Such a confession of faith was a risky defiance of what the Nazi regime was saying and doing.

Third, in 1935 Bonhoeffer began to direct small ministerial training schools sponsored by the Confessing Church, especially one at Finkenwalde. There, as he moved into his thirties, he insisted that his students not only study theology, but also discipline themselves to pray and meditate on scripture. In that setting he wrote several books which have become classics. *The Cost of Discipleship* (1937), currently published as *Discipleship*, contrasts the "cheap grace" of the majority with the "costly grace" of those who take up the cross to follow Jesus.

Life Together (1939), a small book emerging from the same environment, challenged his students and the larger church to authentic Christ-centered community. "Christianity means community through Jesus Christ and in Jesus Christ.... We belong to one another only through and in Jesus Christ" [*Life Together*, trans. by John W. Doberstein (London: SCM Press, 1954), p. 10]. At a time when families, churches, and the nation were being wrenched apart, this came as a special challenge.

While teaching at Finkenwalde, Bonhoeffer briefly met Maria von Wedemeyer. She was an attractive, intelligent seventeen-year-old half his age. But soon the authorities learned of the school, and the police closed it in 1940. Most of the students were forced into the German military and ordered to the front, where they died.

Friends in the United States were concerned for the young theologian and the tightrope he was walking. After much negotiating they were able to offer him a position on the faculty of Union Theological Seminary, where he had studied a decade earlier. But only a month after arriving in New York he changed his mind. He explained his about-face in a famous statement: "I shall have no right to participate in the reconstruction of Christian life in Germany after the war if I do not share the trials of this time with my people." So, to the fears of his American friends, he turned his back on security and returned to almost certain suffering.

Back in Germany Bonhoeffer, a pacifist by inclination, was now forbidden to publish or speak anywhere in the country. He was allowed, however, to serve as a courier for the military intelligence service. Because he already had contacts with leaders of the ecumenical movement in a handful of countries, his brother-in-law, Hans von Dohnanyi, recruited him to use his position to help the underground resistance, and so Bonhoeffer became a double agent. He moved in the highest circles of international conversation between churches. At the same time, opponents of Hitler in the military intelligence welcomed his cooperation as he traveled to Switzerland, Sweden, and Great Britain. In 1942 he carried to Britain terms of surrender which the German military underground felt they could live with. But American and British leaders had already agreed that Germany must be forced into unconditional surrender. Now many in the resistance concluded that the only remaining alternative was to assassinate Hitler.

Dietrich and his friend Maria von Wedemeyer began serious acquaintance and letter-writing in the summer of 1942. At first he was "Pastor Bonhoeffer," but that soon changed. His mind was changing too on issues of faith and responsibility. "I'm not religious by nature," he wrote to a friend, "but I can't help thinking all the time of God, of Christ. I'm greatly devoted to sincerity, to life, liberty and mercy – it's just their religious trappings that make me uneasy." Dietrich and Maria became engaged early in 1943 and then in April he, his sister Christel, and her husband Hans were arrested at his parents' home. Bonhoeffer was charged with suspicious activity (among other things, helping Jews to escape) and draft evasion.

For the next year and a half, he was imprisoned in Tegel, a suburb of Berlin. Maria was allowed to make occasional visits, and they wrote to one another as often as they could. They agreed "it was courage that brought us here," and she saved the letters she got from Dietrich. He also wrote other letters, poems, and meditations which later were published as *Letters and Papers from Prison* – a third classic in the minds of many. This poignant volume offers a glimpse into Bonhoeffer's questions, struggles, and dreams for a way forward after the war. "The church is the church only when it exists for others," he wrote. "The church must share in the secular problems of ordinary human life, not dominating, but helping and serving them."

Although he was not directly connected with the Valkyrie conspiracy to assassinate Hitler in July 1944, he knew of the plot. Those who directly participated were quickly rounded up and executed. Then papers discovered in September revealed that Bonhoeffer was indirectly involved, so he was transferred to a Gestapo prison in Berlin. Now correspondence was forbidden. Twenty-year-old Maria repeatedly tried to visit him, but she never saw him again. In February 1945 he was secretly moved to the infamous concentration camp at Buchenwald. By now the Nazi regime was collapsing. Internally it was in disarray while externally the Allied armies were pushing relentlessly toward Berlin. As they approached the capital they were discovering the horrors of the camps and liberating those who remained in them.

On April 3 several prisoners, some of them high-ranking military officers in the resistance, were transported into the Bavarian Forest to a secluded camp at Flossenburg. This was not a "concentration" camp, but a death camp. When Bonhoeffer's name was called to board the truck, he said to a fellow-prisoner, "This is the end – for me, the beginning of life." With the American army closing in on Flossenburg, a quick court-martial during the night of April 8-9 sentenced Bonhoeffer to death. Early in the morning he was led to the gallows, ordered to strip naked, and hanged. Not many days afterward one of his brothers and two brothers-in-law also died for their part in the resistance. Within days the Americans liberated Flossenburg, the German high command surrendered, and the war in Europe was over. Only then did faithful Maria learn what had happened to her fiancé.

Four years later Bonhoeffer's book *The Cost of Discipleship* appeared in English translation, and the world began to learn of the young pastor-professor who was martyred at thirty-nine. Maria continued her studies in Germany and then made her way to the United States. A mathematician by training, she had a successful career in the new computer industry until she was diagnosed with cancer in an advanced stage. She died in 1977 at the age of fifty-three. In her final months Maria entrusted to her sister the letters she had received more than thirty years earlier from Dietrich. The sister kept them as a family treasure but finally allowed them to be published as *Love Letters from Cell 92* (1995).

Bonhoeffer's theology has been the object of much discussion and speculation. He was a brilliant thinker, schooled in classical liberalism, who moved in a new direction quite his own. But no one can doubt the faith and courage with which he approached both life and death. His commitment to Christ and willingness to act for others give him an honored place among the church's heroes. He lived out his own famous statement, "When Christ calls a man, he bids him come and die."

In Bonhoeffer's Voice

The Cost of Discipleship, written in 1937 while Bonhoeffer was leading the little secret seminary, is an exposition of the Sermon on the Mount and the other discourses of Jesus in Matthew's Gospel. It is also a stinging indictment of a church that has become over-confident and all too comfortable. The first chapter of his best-known book contrasts what Bonhoeffer called cheap churchly grace and costly biblical grace.

Grace Costly grace is the gospel which must be sought again and again, the gift which must be asked for, the door at which we must knock. Such grace is costly because it calls us to follow, and it is grace because it calls us to follow Jesus Christ. It is costly because it costs us our life, and it is grace because it gives us the only true life. It is costly because it condemns sin, and grace because it justifies the sinner. Above all, it is costly because it cost God the life of his Son: 'you were bought with a price,' and what has cost God much cannot be cheap for us. Above all, it is grace because God did not reckon his Son too dear a price to pay for our life, but delivered him up for us. Costly grace is the Incarnation of God.

. . . The price we are having to pay today in the shape of the collapse of the organized church is only the inevitable consequence of our policy of making grace available to all at too low a cost. . . . We poured forth unending streams of grace. But the call to follow Jesus in the narrow way was hardly ever heard. . . . What had happened to all those warnings of Luther's against preaching the gospel in such a manner as to make people rest secure in their ungodly living? . . . With us it has been abundantly proved that the sins of the fathers are visited upon the children unto the third and fourth generations. Cheap grace has turned out to be utterly merciless to our Evangelical Church [Dietrich Bonhoeffer, *The Cost of Discipleship*, trans. by R. H. Fuller (London: SCM Press, second ed., 1959), chap. 1, alt.].

While Bonhoeffer was wrestling with his identity as a German and his subsequent martyrdom, C.S. Lewis was living in Great Britain, and teaching at Oxford. His journey to faith involved a long search and the sidecar of a motorcycle.

17

APOSTLE TO THE SKEPTICS

C. S. LEWIS

How do you play a word game like Scrabble with someone who has photographic memory? They can recall everything they have ever read. And what if the rules allow them to use words from any language they know? That was the way Jack and Joy Lewis played the game. Both could read English, French, Greek, and Latin – and both had almost total recall! The world knows them by their professional names, Joy Davidman and C. S. Lewis. Yet to those who knew them personally he was Jack, she was his Joy, and for a few blissful, cruel years they were husband and wife.

The story began in 1895 with the birth of Warren Hamilton Lewis in Belfast, Northern Ireland, and then his brother Clive Staples Lewis in 1898. They were the sons of lawyer Albert Lewis and his wife Florence (Flora), brothers who would be inseparable throughout their lives. At the age of four Clive announced that he was to be called "Jacksie," and the nickname Jack stuck. It was clear that he was intelligent, for he had considerable knowledge of Greek and Latin by the age of six. He also sensed a longing for something he could not name – beauty perhaps, or joy.

His mother's death from cancer when he was nine destroyed his childhood security, and his restless father sent him off to a series of boarding schools. Some of these were ineptly run, and one especially cruel headmaster was later declared mentally unfit. By age fifteen Jack concluded that he was an atheist chiefly interested in the myths of Scandinavia – Odin, Thor, Valhalla, and such. Then into his life came William T. Kirkpatrick, the teacher chiefly responsible for what the boy became. Called "the great Knock" behind his back, his task was to prepare Jack to compete for a scholarship to a prestigious university. Kirkpatrick, an avowed atheist, was famous for his relentless logic which chiseled, sanded, and polished the abilities of his pupil.

Together they succeeded, and in the spring of 1917 Jack Lewis enrolled at University College, founded in 1280, one of the oldest of forty schools which comprise the University of Oxford. But his studies were cut short because Great Britain was in the middle of World War I. Lewis entered the officer training program and reached the front lines in France on his nineteenth birthday, November 29, 1917. Several months later he was wounded by shrapnel and endured a long recuperation. By that time, he had decided that religion was all myth and composed his first published work, *Death in Battle*.

His closest buddy in the army was fellow Irishman E. F. C. (Paddy) Moore. Together they agreed that if either of them should be killed, the other would care for the deceased friend's parents. Paddy went missing in action, and at the war's end he was declared dead. When Lewis resumed his schooling, he also assumed the care of Paddy's mother and his sister Maureen. They moved to Oxford, and Jack lived with them. Eventually as Mrs. Moore aged she became ever-more demanding, and he became her virtual servant. This arrangement continued for more than thirty years until her death in 1951, when Lewis was fifty-three.

After university, Warren (Warnie) Lewis chose military service as his career while Jack continued his own studies at Oxford. He garnered a series of "firsts" in Greek and Latin literature (1920), philosophy and ancient history (1922), and English (1923). From then on, classics, philosophy, and literature would be his professional world. Although he initially taught philosophy for one year, Oxford's Magdalen College (pronounced Maudlin) hired him for English language and literature, a position he held for the remainder of his career there. In 1930 Warren, between military assignments, helped the Moores and Jack move into The Kilns, a large, rambling house near an old brickyard at the edge of Oxford. There Lewis could study, think, write, take long walks, and swim in a small lake – all of which he loved to do.

Yet his inner life was conflicted. The boyhood atheist and adult agnostic had become a theist in 1929 with his admission "God is God." Still searching, he was troubled by the human desire for pleasure, beauty, and joy. He began to read the Greek New Testament in light of other writings he had studied and taught. Concluding that the Gospels report real history rather than myth, he knew he must become a fully decided Christian. It happened in 1931 on a trip to the zoo with Warnie, who owned a motorcycle. Jack rode in the sidecar and – as he reported it – "When we set out I did not believe that Jesus Christ was the Son of God, and when we reached the zoo I did."

The decision came after long talks with fellow professors who were both Christians and experts in their academic fields. Chief among them were H. V. D. (Hugo) Dyson and J. R. R. Tolkien, today world famous through his fantasy fiction. Both men spent a long night shortly before the zoo trip trying to persuade Lewis to embrace Christianity. With his decision in place, they began to meet regularly with others in 1933 for conversation – often debate – and to try out their newest writing on one another. Because the group centered around their love of literature, they dubbed themselves the Inklings. This informal community of Christian scholars became one of the most important influences in Lewis's life until his death thirty years later.

England entered World War II in September 1939, and later the nightly bombings of London began. In a drastic maneuver, thousands of children were taken from their homes and moved to safety outside the capital. As part of this project, the Lewis-Moore household in Oxford welcomed into their midst several girls evacuated from London. His brother Warren shipped out to France where he became one of the British troops rescued from Dunkirk in 1940. Later career assignments took him to Sierra Leone in West Africa and to Shanghai, China. When he retired from the reserves in 1947, he held the rank of major.

C. S. Lewis's writing during the thirties was mostly scholarly in nature, for which he received praise and several prizes. Then in 1941 *The Guardian* newspaper began to print a fictitious correspondence from a senior demon (Screwtape) to a younger one (Wormwood), instructing him on how to capture and kill a Christian. When collected into a book, *The Screwtape Letters* proved to be one of Lewis's most popular works. He found it difficult to write because he had to think backwards (the Enemy is God), but it is an insightful, serious treatment of how temptation works. From then on, Lewis's writing was both his major activity and his chief recreation.

His popularity led to an invitation from the BBC radio network: would he – a combat veteran – prepare a series of mid-war talks explaining Christian faith to military personnel who were not theologians, maybe not even Christians? He responded in 1942 with *Broadcast Talks* (also called *The Case for Christianity*), followed by *Christian Behaviour* (1943) and *Beyond Personality: or First Steps in the Doctrine of the Trinity* (1944). These were all combined in 1952 into the book *Mere Christianity*. One recent poll of literary reviewers voted it the twentieth century's most influential Christian book.

The years 1940-60 saw a flood of writing pour from the pen of the Oxford professor. It came in more literary forms than perhaps any other well-known author's work. Lewis produced lay theology, apologetics, science fiction, poetry, literary criticism, children's fiction, essays, book reviews, and psychological novels. There seemed to be no end to what his imagination could conceive. *Time* magazine featured him in its cover article on September 8, 1947. It described him tongue-in-cheek as an intellectual whose heresy was Christianity. One of the first books about Lewis dubbed him "the apostle to the skeptics." Several universities recognized his outstanding work by awarding him honorary doctor's degrees.

All was not well at Oxford. Lewis was now writing a series of children's books, *The Chronicles of Narnia* (1950-56), which were widely acclaimed. Some of the faculty, however, felt he was demeaning scholarship by such activity. Lewis did, in fact, produce scholarly material that was brilliant, but they wanted more. So, in 1954, when Cambridge University offered a position created just for him, he accepted it. He could continue to live at The Kilns, commuting each week by train to teach at Cambridge. His years there proved to be both fruitful and fulfilling.

During this time his personal life took an unexpected turn. Because his writing had become so popular, he received stacks of mail each week. Warnie, now retired from the army, helped with the letter writing because Jack was determined that every piece received must be answered. One correspondent was an American writer named Joy Davidman Gresham. Jewish by birth and a former Marxist, she had become a Christian through reading Lewis's books. Her marriage had dissolved, so she and her sons David and Douglas (ages eleven and ten) moved to England. There she met Lewis, and they became good friends. She was brilliant, brassy, and bold – Lewis's match in nearly everything. They played Scrabble with one game board, two sets of letters, and any word they ever read in any language.

Eventually she and her sons were threatened with deportation from the country. The British government would not renew their visas as visitors. In a move no one could have foreseen, the fifty-seven-year-old bachelor proposed that his friend marry him. For Lewis there was nothing romantic about it – it was a totally rational idea. By marrying him, Joy and her sons would be allowed to remain in England. She and Jack would continue to live separately and just be friends. In April 1956 they were united in a civil ceremony, but told no one about it. Six months later, however, Joy was diagnosed with advanced bone cancer and given only a short time to live. Lewis now insisted they must have a fully Christian wedding because he intended to care for her sons after she died, but a Christian wedding meant they had to go public. At Christmas they disclosed their earlier civil marriage with a small announcement in *The Times* of London. It is almost trivial to say that Jack's colleagues and friends were shocked. In their eyes his action was scandalous, and Lewis paid dearly in the loss of personal relationships.

Their civil marriage held, and in March 1957 the Reverend Peter Bide, one of Jack's former pupils, came to Joy's hospital room and joined them in a Christian wedding ceremony. Bide had a reputation as a healer, and Lewis asked him to pray and lay hands on Joy. He did so, and within months she was walking again. A year later her cancer was in remission, and The Kilns was her new home. It didn't take her long to spruce up both house and husband. Lewis had earlier written *Surprised by Joy*, an autobiography describing his life up to his conversion. Now, to his astonished delight, he was surprised by his love for his wife. She was indeed his Joy, and their marriage was deeply satisfying for them both.

In the summer of 1958, they honeymooned in his native Ireland, but late the next year her disease returned. Still, they were able to fulfill a longstanding dream when they toured Greece in the spring of 1960. Joy was in pain, but she managed to walk, tramp, and climb throughout their visit. When she returned to England her condition rapidly worsened, and she died three months later at home in The Kilns at the age of forty-five. "The night before she died," Jack later wrote, "we had a long, quiet, nourishing, and tranquil talk." Joy had asked to be cremated, and her funeral was extremely painful for the Lewis brothers. The only people present were Jack, Warren, Joy's two sons, the Anglican priest who conducted the service, and his wife (both close friends). Warnie noted in his diary that "none of J[ack]'s friends bothered to put in [an] appearance." Their marriage was still not approved in Lewis's Oxford circle.

Joy's death shook Jack to the foundations of his faith. True to his craft, he wrote to work through his loss. The result was *A Grief Observed*, supposedly written by "N. W. Clerk." Only after his own death did the world learn that the real author of this poignant, powerful book was C. S. Lewis. In the opinion of many, it remains one of the best books written about the anguish of the death of a loved one. A stage play and two film versions of it have appeared, all of them titled *Shadowlands*.

Shortly before the book was published Lewis was diagnosed with a severe prostate condition, too advanced for surgery. The next two years saw continuing care for his stepsons, retirement from teaching, a major heart attack, a stay in a nursing home, and his return to The Kilns. He knew he was dying but maintained a realistic outlook and his good humor to the end. It came on November 22, 1963, just one week before his sixty-fifth birthday. On the same day President John F. Kennedy was killed in Dallas, Texas. In the confusion and grief that followed, most Americans and many in Great Britain failed to notice any news reporting the death of the famous writer in Oxford.

He was laid to rest at his parish church with an epitaph which Warren composed: "IN LOVING MEMORY OF MY BROTHER, CLIVE STAPLES LEWIS, BORN BELFAST 29th NOVEMBER 1898, DIED IN THIS PARISH 22nd NOVEMBER 1963. *MEN MUST ENDURE THEIR GOING HENCE"* [a quotation from Shakespeare's *King Lear*]. As before, only a handful of acquaintances attended the funeral. Warnie, devastated at losing Jack, succumbed to his lifelong battle with alcohol and stayed away. In the absence of any blood relative, Maureen Moore and Lewis's two stepsons accompanied his coffin to the cemetery.

Major Warren Lewis died ten years later at The Kilns. Maureen Moore, by then Lady Dunbar of Hempriggs, lived until 1997. Today David Gresham follows the faith of his birth family as an Orthodox Jew. Douglas Gresham, a Christian actively involved in fostering his stepfather's legacy, has written, "Jack was the finest man and best Christian I have ever known. I loved him and dearly cherish his memory."

Shortly before he died C. S. Lewis composed and dictated an epitaph for his wife. It was placed in the crematorium where she was interred. "Remember HELEN JOY DAVIDMAN, D. July 1960, Loved wife of C. S. Lewis."

Here the whole world (stars, water, air,
And field, and forest, as they were
Reflected in a single mind)
Like cast off clothes was left behind
In ashes, yet with hope that she,
Re-born from holy poverty,
In lenten lands, hereafter may
Resume them on her Easter Day.

Today, almost five decades after his death, C. S. Lewis's books sell about two million copies each year. Although in some ways a romanticist, he was first known as a defender of Christianity through such writings as *Mere Christianity, The Problem of Pain*, and *God in the Dock*. He tackled difficult topics such as miracles, grief, kinds of love and, in *The Screwtape Letters*, temptation. Multitudes of readers relish the subtle meanings in his seven volumes of children's stories (*The Chronicles of Narnia*). Others prefer his science fiction trilogy or the imaginative novel *Till We Have Faces* (his personal favorite among his books). Still others enjoy his original poetry and his technical, scholarly expertise in medieval and Renaissance English.

Lewis was by turns a self-styled atheist, an instructor in philosophy, a professor of literature, an avid hiker, a literary critic, an expert on mythology, a fierce public debater, a BBC radio speaker, a mentor of students, a faithful member of the Church of England, and a warm, garrulous friend. A famous American fundamentalist spent some time with him and later allegedly said, "That man drinks alcohol and smokes tobacco, but I believe he is a Christian!" For reasons of their own, a host of readers around the world will agree.

In Lewis' Voice

C. S. Lewis did not write devotional books as such, but his writings continue to illuminate and inspire. Here are three notable passages selected from the three decades of his most productive work. The first is from his sermon "The Weight of Glory," which he preached in June 1941 to one of the largest congregations ever assembled in Oxford's most famous church. This is the conclusion of that remarkable address.

No Ordinary People. There are no ordinary people. You have never talked to a mere mortal. Nations, cultures, arts, civilizations – these are mortal, and their life is to ours as the life of a gnat. But it is immortals whom we joke with, work with, marry, snub, and exploit – immortal horrors or everlasting splendors. This does not mean that we are to be perpetually solemn. We must play. But our merriment must be of that kind (and it is, in fact, the merriest kind) which exists between people who have, from the outset, taken each other seriously – no flippancy, no superiority, no presumption. And our charity must be a real and costly love, with deep feeling for the sins in spite of which we love the sinner – no mere tolerance, or indulgence which parodies love as flippancy parodies merriment.

Next to the Blessed Sacrament itself, your neighbor is the holiest object presented to your senses. If he is your Christian neighbor, he is holy in almost the same way, for in him also Christ . . . – the glorifier and the glorified, Glory Himself, is truly hidden [C. S. Lewis, *The Weight of Glory and Other Addresses* (HarperSanFrancisco, 2001), p. 46, spelling Americanized].

The Screwtape Letters (1942) and *Mere Christianity* (1952), sometimes published together, may be Lewis's most popular single books. In the latter he discusses Christian marriage in his own inimitable way.

Being In Love. What we call 'being in love' is a glorious state, and, in several ways, good for us. . . . Being in love is a good thing, but it is not the best thing. There are many things below it, but there are also things above it. You cannot make it the basis of a whole life. It is a noble feeling, but it is still a feeling. Now no feeling can be relied on to last in its full intensity, or even to last at all. Knowledge can last, principles can last, habits can last; but feelings come and go. And in fact, whatever people say, the state called 'being in love' usually does not last. . . . But, of course, ceasing to be 'in love' need not mean ceasing to love. Love in this second sense – love as distinct from 'being in love' is not merely a feeling. It is a deep unity, maintained by the will and deliberately strengthened by habit; reinforced by (in Christian marriages) the grace which both parents ask, and receive, from God. . . . 'Being in love' first moved them to promise fidelity: this quieter love enables them to keep the promise. It is on this love that the engine of marriage is run: being in love was the explosion that started it [C. S. Lewis, *Mere Christianity* (New York: The Macmillan Company, 1960), p. 84f.].

The last book C. S. Lewis prepared for the press was *Letters to: Chiefly on Prayer*. Published after his death, it was another fictitious correspondence, this time with an imaginary friend Malcolm, the husband of Betty and father of George. Listen in on Lewis:

To Pray.   What we must fight against is [Alexander] Pope's maxim the first Almighty Cause Acts not by partial, but by general laws.

. . . I will not believe in the Managerial God and his general laws. If there is Providence at all, everything is providential and every providence is a special providence. It is an old and pious saying that Christ died not only for Man but for each man, just as much as if each had been the only man there was. Can I not believe the same of this creative act – which, as spread out in time, we call destiny or history? It is for the sake of each human soul. Each is an end. Perhaps for each beast. Perhaps even each particle of matter – the night sky suggests that the inanimate also has for God some value we cannot imagine. His ways are not (not there, anyway) like ours.

If you ask why I believe all this, I can only reply that we are taught, both by precept and example, to pray, and that prayer would be meaningless in the sort of universe Pope pictured. One of the purposes for which God instituted prayer may have been to bear witness that the course of events is not governed like a state but created like a work of art to which every being makes its contribution and (in prayer) a conscious contribution, and in which every being is both an end and a means. And since I have momentarily considered prayer itself as a means let me hasten to add that it is also an end. The world was made partly that there might be prayer; partly that our prayers for George might be answered. But let's have finished with 'partly.' The great work of art was made for the sake of all it does and is, down to the curve of every wave and the flight of every insect [C. S. Lewis, *Letters to Malcolm: Chiefly on Prayer* (New York: Harcourt, Brace & World, 1963), pp. 53, 55f.].

Our more recent spiritual companions have come from the Protestant tradition; our next friend, also from the twentieth century, is the Roman Catholic monk Thomas Merton.

18

A MERRY, MISCHIEVOUS MONK

THOMAS MERTON

Some experts have called Thomas Merton the twentieth century's most important Catholic spiritual writer. Notre Dame professor Lawrence Cunningham, a friend of Merton, described him as " . . . a monk by vocation, a theologian by conviction, and a writer by instinct" [*Thomas Merton: Spiritual Master* (New York: Paulist Press, 1992), p. 32]. Brilliant, youthfully wild, and always witty, another friend, William H. Shannon called him "a merry, mischievous monk." All of this is accurate, but it seems impossible to catch and hold all the qualities of this remarkable man.

Thomas Feverel Merton was born January 31, 1915, in southern France to parents who were artists. His New Zealand father and American mother had met and married in London, then moved to France. From birth until young adulthood his life was marked by loss – loss of a place that he might call home and loss of persons dear to him. When he was one year old his parents brought him to New York, where his brother John Paul was born in 1918. From the outset Thomas showed exceptional intelligence, able to read and write by the age of five. But his mother died when Tom was six, and he turned to his paternal grandmother for emotional support. His father, searching for places where he could do landscape painting, took the boys back to France, then moved to England where he died when Tom was sixteen. The orphaned teenager won a scholarship to Cambridge University, but after one year he was dismissed. He had been drunk too many times, and there were allegations he had caused an extra-marital pregnancy.

Returning to the U.S., he attended Columbia University, graduating in 1938. During that time, he experienced more loss as both of his grandfathers died. Except for his brother and a circle of friends, he was now alone in the world. A popular, gifted student with an interest in art, he became editor of the university's yearbook. At the suggestion of one of his teachers, a Hindu, he began to study Augustine's *Confessions* and *The Imitation of Christ*. The insight and wisdom of these classics had a profound impact on the young man, and at twenty-three he joined the Catholic Church. Continuing at Columbia, he received a master's degree for his research on the artist and mystic William Blake.

He planned to go on for a Ph.D. focusing on the Jesuit poet Gerard Manley Hopkins. First, however, he spent two years teaching English at St. Bonaventure University in Olean, New York. The school was run by the Franciscans, and Merton decided to apply for admission to the Order. But his past followed him, and the Franciscans said no. Convinced he was called to be a monk, he turned to one of the most severe Orders in the church, Cistercians of the Strict Observance, or Trappists. He applied to their monastery at Gethsemani, Kentucky, where he had earlier gone on retreat, and was accepted. At twenty-six he had at last found a place he could call home and a community that would become his family.

Life in the Trappist monastery was a disciplined, austere existence. The general rule was silence, abstinence from meat, fish and eggs, prayers in the chapel around 2:00 a.m., common dormitories for sleeping on plank beds, and mandatory manual labor. Above all there was the Divine Office, a series of prayer services at stated hours seven times each day.

Two years into his monastic life, Merton learned that his brother John Paul had been killed in World War II. He was a pilot for the Royal Canadian Air Force and was shot down over Mannheim, Germany. At twenty-eight, Tom's only family now was his monastic brothers. Knowing of Merton's unusual background, the abbot asked him to write his autobiography, which he finished by the time he was thirty-three. *The Seven Storey Mountain* reads in some ways like a modern version of Augustine's *Confessions*. It became an international sensation, selling six hundred thousand hardback copies in the United States alone. The story of the transient, troubled young man appealed to many readers, but in the monastery he was content. There, at thirty-four, he was ordained to the priesthood, receiving the name Father Louis, and in 1951 he became an American citizen.

The years that followed were busy ones for the monk. He read widely and began to correspond with intellectuals in many countries. His superiors affirmed his obvious abilities and assigned him to teach a variety of subjects to the newer monks. He also wrote, primarily contemplative and monastic works, until age forty-five. He graded his books, and by his own reckoning the best from this period were *The Sign of Jonas, No Man Is an Island, Thoughts in Solitude, The Wisdom of the Desert,* and what some consider in its revised form to be his finest work, *New Seeds of Contemplation.*

Another book, *Disputed Questions,* signaled a transition in Merton's thinking. Now in his mid-forties, he was more open to currents of modern life and world problems. He believed that union with God was not for monastics only, but for everyone, and in the ordinary duties and challenges of life. Writing on both religious and intellectual questions, he began to critique America's consumerism, militarism, and racism. This was the 1960s, a time of profound cultural change, and he listed among his better books *The Way of Chuang Tzu, Raids on the Unspeakable,* and *Conjectures of a Guilty Bystander.*

At last, at fifty, after years of asking, he was allowed to live alone in a small concrete-block house on the monastery grounds. Its greater isolation gave him opportunity to pursue contacts in other religions, their monastic practice, and monastic ways in general. From his hermitage Merton was in touch with a dizzying array of famous people who wrote to him. Among them were the Nicaraguan poet Ernesto Cardenal (formerly a novice under Merton's instruction), Russian novelist Boris Pasternak (author of *Doctor Zhivago*), noted Buddhist teachers D. T. Suzuki and Thic Nhat Hanh, John Howard Griffin (author of *Black like Me*), Catholic philosopher Jacques Maritain, and civil rights leader Martin Luther King, Jr.

In 1968 his superiors gave permission for him to speak at an international conference on monasticism in Bangkok, Thailand. Traveling by way of India, he met with the Dalai Lama before proceeding on to the conference. At the close of his address he noted that there would be opportunity for questions and discussion later in the day, so he would just "disappear for a while." Several hours later a shout was reported from the vicinity of Merton's lodging. When people began to investigate, they found him lying on the floor partially clothed with electrical burns on his body. On top of him lay an electric fan about five feet tall which proved to have defective wiring.

No one can say with precision just what had happened. One explanation is that he touched the fan while his body was damp and the current short-circuited to cause a fatal heart attack. It was December 10, 1968, twenty-seven years to the day since he had entered Gethsemani. Merton was fifty-three. His body was flown back to the monastery where his brother monks buried it in the communal cemetery. His grave's cross-shaped marker, uniform with all the others, reads simply, "Father Louis Merton, 1915-1968."

Although Merton's life was cut short, he left behind much unpublished writing – more words, in fact, than in the entire Bible. In the generation since his death a stream of books by him and about him has appeared. Among those which he himself wrote are *Contemplative Prayer*, *Contemplation in a World of Action*, and *The Asian Journal of Thomas Merton* (edited by others). By prior arrangement with the monastery, his private journals were sealed for twenty-five years after his death. They now have been published, all seven volumes of them. It is no surprise he once joked that he was born with a pencil in his hand!

Thomas Merton is without question America's most famous monk. Although he belonged to a contemplative Order in the church, he was in touch with the world. He felt especially connected when he was most alone because he believed in the deep prayer that arises out of disciplined solitude and silence. And he maintained that meaningful social action would grow out of silence. Professor Cunningham was right: Merton was a monk by calling, a theologian by conviction, and a writer by instinct. Countless readers – Catholics, Protestants, and Orthodox – have found in him a wise, profound spiritual master, a guide in the things of God.

In Merton's Voice

Deciding where to start in reading Thomas Merton can be a challenge, but one small, accessible book is *Thoughts in Solitude* (1958). Written during 1953-54, it contains reflections from the period when he was most focused on his own monastic life. He divided his thoughts into two parts: (1) aspects of the spiritual life and (2) the love of solitude. Here are several passages from the second part.

Solitude. Let this be my only consolation, that wherever I am, You, my Lord, are loved and praised.

The trees indeed love You without knowing You. The tiger lilies and corn flowers are there, proclaiming that they love You, without being aware of Your presence. The beautiful dark clouds ride slowly across the sky musing on You like children who do not know what they are dreaming of, as they play.

But in the midst of them all, I know You, and I know of Your presence. In them and in me I know of the love which they do not know, and, what is greater, I am abashed by the presence of Your love in me. O kind and terrible love, which You have given me, and which could never be in my heart if You did not love me! For in the midst of these beings which have never offended You, I am loved by You, and it would seem most of all as one who has offended You. I am seen by You under the sky, and my offenses have been forgotten by You – but I have not forgotten them.

Only one thing I ask: that the memory of them should not make me afraid to receive into my heart the gift of Love – which You have placed in me. I will receive it because I am unworthy. In doing so I will only love You all the more, and give Your mercy greater glory.

Remembering that I have been a sinner, I will love You in spite of what I have been, knowing that my love is precious because it is Yours, rather than my own. Precious to You because it comes from Your own Son, but precious even more because it makes me Your child [Thomas Merton, *Thoughts in Solitude* (New York: Farrar, Straus and Giroux, 1958), p. 99f.].

The Father's Love. Father, I love You whom I do not know, and I embrace You whom I do not see, and I abandon myself to You whom I have offended, because You love in me Your only begotten Son. You see him in me, You embrace him in me, because he has willed to identify himself completely with me by that love which brought him to death, for me, on the Cross.

I come to you like Jacob in the garments of Esau, that is in the merits and the precious blood of Jesus Christ. And You, Father, who have willed to be as though blind in the darkness of this great mystery which is the revelation of Your love, pass Your hands over my head, and bless me as Your only Son. You have willed to see me only in him, but in willing this You have willed to see me really as I am. For the sinful self is not my real self, it is not the self You have wanted for me, only the self that I have wanted for myself. And I no longer want this false self. But now, Father, I come to you in your own Son's self, for it is his sacred heart that has taken possession of me and destroyed my sins and it is he who presents me to You. And where? In the sanctuary of his own heart, which is Your palace and the temple where the saints adore You in heaven [Thomas Merton, *Thoughts in Solitude* (New York: Farrar, Straus and Girous, 1958), p. 71f.].

The Desire to Please God. My Lord God, I have no idea where I am going. I do not see the road ahead of me. I cannot know for certain where it will end. Nor do I really know myself, and the fact that I think I am following your will does not mean that I am actually doing so. But I believe that the desire to please you does in fact please you. And I hope I have that desire in all that I am doing. I hope that I will never do anything apart from that desire. And I know that if I do this you will lead me by the right road, though I may know nothing about it. Therefore I will trust you always though I may seem to be lost and in the shadow of death. I will not fear, for you are ever with me, and you will never leave me to face my perils alone [Thomas Merton, *Thoughts in Solitude* (New York: Farrar, Straus and Giroux, 1958), p. 83].

Thomas Merton chose the way of disciplined solitude, while our final friend, also a Roman Catholic, found his way to God in the midst of an academic career and life in L'Arche. Welcome, Henri Nouwen.

19

WOUNDED HEALER

HENRI NOUWEN

Japanese artist Yushi Nomura visited Yale Divinity School in the spring of 1978. The prospective student was reading a bulletin board filled with announcements and ads when someone approached him. The man was middle-aged, with shaggy hair and rumpled clothes. "Hi," he said, "I'm Henry. What's your name?" Thinking he must be the janitor, Nomura warmed as the man smiled and extended his hand. "I'm Yushi," the young visitor replied. The janitor shook his hand vigorously, saying, "Nice meeting you here, Yushi." Then he turned and walked back the way he had come. He may be a little odd, thought Nomura, but still he seemed like a nice guy.

That autumn Yushi Nomura began his studies at Yale and made sure he got to class early the first day. All the seats filled quickly, and overflow students stood around the walls. Yushi felt reassured when he saw the janitor at the front erasing the chalkboard. "Go, Henry, go," he said to himself. "You better finish it quick, for the professor will arrive at any moment." With his cleaning completed, the janitor then began to write fresh words on the board – large words, technical terms. Nomura was confused, so he asked the student next to him, "Who is he?" The answer came back, "That's Professor Nouwen, of course."

For ten years Professor Henri J.M. Nouwen, who just wanted to be called "Henry," was one of Yale Divinity School's most popular professors. His knowledge and personality combined to crowd his classroom with eager learners. His compassionate, gentle wisdom attracted and held those who listened to him. His books did the same as readers came to feel a close connection with this somewhat odd, very nice guy. People occasionally did mistake him for a homeless person, and he remains one of the most beloved Christian figures of the twentieth century.

That century was marked by restless movement and runaway change. Nouwen's life also was filled with restlessness, movement, and change. He was born Henri Jozef Machiel Nouwen on January 24, 1932, in the Netherlands. His mother was a warm, affirming presence in his life, but for many years he and his lawyer father experienced a strained, competitive relationship. The Nouwens were Catholics, and young Henri always wanted to be a priest. By age eight he had turned their attic into a small chapel where he played at saying mass.

World War II began, and Nazi troops occupied the Netherlands. The Nouwens knew of Jewish neighbors who were being deported, and Henri's father had to hide at times to escape being sent into forced labor. Henri would later refer to the war's final year as "the horrible winter of hunger." Life improved after 1945, and at nineteen he entered seminary to prepare for the priesthood, receiving ordination at twenty-five. His abilities and interests convinced his superiors to let him study psychology for seven years at the University of Nijmegen. He followed that with two more years as a student fellow at the Menninger Foundation in Topeka, Kansas.

With that impressive background, in 1966 Notre Dame University invited him to teach psychology. During his two years there he pioneered by offering courses in abnormal psychology and by asking Protestants to lecture in his classes. Returning to the Netherlands, he spent two years as a staff member and teacher at Catholic institutes and another year back at Nijmegen as a doctoral student. His academic work was informed and sensitive, but he would not write in the detached, formal style that was expected, so he received the degree "doctorandus" – almost a doctor.

At this time Yale Divinity School hired the thirty-nine-year-old Dutchman as an associate professor of pastoral psychology. He taught courses in two areas: ministry and spirituality. The dean affirmed Henri's special gifts and training and allowed him privileges not granted to other teachers. Chief among them, he could write non-academic books. He received tenure on the faculty and in 1977 was promoted to full professor. With one later exception, his decade at Yale was the longest time Nouwen ever spent in one place in his adult life. That's when he met and befriended Yushi Nomura. Soon after, the two combined their talents to produce *Wisdom from the Desert: Sayings from the Desert Fathers*, which features delightful drawings by the Japanese artist.

Along with his teaching Nouwen was proving to be a wise, insightful writer, producing thirteen books in those ten years. He believed that what is most personal is most universal, and readers seemed to welcome the very personal quality of his writing. Some of the best-known books from his Yale years were *With Open Hands; The Wounded Healer: Ministry in Contemporary Society; Reaching Out: The Three Movements of the Spiritual Life;* and *The Way of the Heart: Desert Spirituality and Contemporary Ministry.*

Nouwen's restlessness caught up with him, and he left Yale in 1981 to become a family brother at the Abbey of the Genesee in upstate New York. This large, well-known monastery belongs to the Trappists, Thomas Merton's Order. The monks welcomed Nouwen as a fellow worshiper in their daily prayers and as a fellow worker in the bakery. Their Monks' Bread is popular, and its sales help to support the monastery. Nouwen also spent six months serving in impoverished areas of Bolivia and Peru, but concluded God had not called him to be a missionary. A constant journaler, he published two books from these times of transition: *The Genesee Diary* and *Gracias! A Latin American Journal.*

He moved again, this time to Harvard Divinity School where he was a popular, beloved figure. In contrast to Thomas Merton, he was now alluding to other religions less and less, focusing almost entirely on the Jesus of the Gospels. His classes drew as many as three hundred students, eager not so much for academic information as for spiritual inspiration. At least once a public lecture by Nouwen was advertised, but far more people came than the room could hold. He asked those who lived in town to return home so the out-of-towners could have seats. For those who lived locally he promised to repeat the lecture at a later date.

But his heart just wasn't in academia, and after only three years he resigned in 1985. Now, by his own choice, he had walked away from three of the world's most prestigious universities – Notre Dame, Yale, and Harvard. Having met Jean Vanier, the founder of L'Arche (the ark), he went to France where he spent nine months at the original L'Arche community. L'Arche communities are homes for people with severe disabilities, distinctive because in them "clients" and their care-takers live together. The sense of closeness, the experience of belonging and being loved, was something Nouwen had searched for through all the restless movements of his life. *The Road to Daybreak*, his journal from this time of transition, would become another of his popular books.

Following his stay in France he visited the famed Hermitage art museum in St. Petersburg, Russia. Over a period of several days he closely studied Rembrandt's large painting "The Return of the Prodigal Son." Always interested in art, Nouwen had felt especially drawn to the work of his fellow countrymen Vincent van Gogh and Rembrandt van Rijn. Nouwen noted the painting's details, observing how they seemed to change as light changed in the room through the day. For several years afterward – painful years – he thought and wrote about his experience. The result was *The Return of the Prodigal Son: A Meditation on Fathers, Brothers, and Sons,* a book he dedicated to his father for his ninetieth birthday. Many people consider it to be the best of his forty books.

In 1986 he was invited to become the full-time live-in chaplain of Daybreak, the L'Arche community in Richmond Hill (Toronto), Ontario, where he stayed for ten years. This was an unprecedented experience for him in which clients gave him the tender, affectionate love that had escaped him – and he responded spontaneously and joyously. He had much to learn, for until now he had led a sheltered life in which much was done for him. Details of how to deal with laundry, manage a refrigerator, and make a sandwich were new challenges. Driving was also. Intensely involved in conversation, he usually drove too slow or too fast. On one famous occasion Daybreak sent him to the airport in a brand-new automobile, but he totaled the car by driving under a semi-trailer! Yet he was so warm and genuine that people were continually drawn to him. The love he received and the love he gave compensated for almost everything missing in his life.

Friendship was desperately important to Nouwen, and he had hundreds of friends near and far. Still, his heart ached for even more closeness, and when one especially close friend pulled away because he found Henri too demanding, the priest spiraled down into clinical depression. For seven months he was away from the Daybreak community under the intensive care of skilled therapists and spiritual directors. The depression was terrible, and each day he wrote notes of encouragement to himself in a private journal. Friends learned of this journal some years later, and reluctantly he allowed them to see what he had written. Insisting this material was so poignant and powerful that others must read it, they urged him to publish the journal. After editing he titled it *The Inner Voice of Love: A Journey Through Anguish to Freedom*. Some reviewers believe it is the most focused, most powerful of all his books, but the public did not learn the story behind it until after his death.

By 1996 *The Return of the Prodigal Son* had become so popular that plans were made for Nouwen to return to the Netherlands, pick up a film crew, and fly to St. Petersburg. There he would be filmed lecturing in front of Rembrandt's six-by-eight-foot painting. But during his stopover in the Netherlands, he suffered a severe heart attack and had to be hospitalized. Friends from the U.S. and Europe flew to his bedside, and he seemed to improve. But several days later a second heart attack proved fatal, and he died in a Dutch hospital on September 21, 1996. It was the day *The Inner Voice of Love* went on sale to the public.

After a funeral in the Netherlands his body was flown back to Toronto where a large funeral featured his wooden casket decorated by the clients with whom he had lived at Daybreak. Twelve hundred people attended the three-hour ecumenical service. He was laid to rest not far from the community where he spent the last, happiest ten years of his life. Since then, biographers narrate his story, scholars analyze his thinking, and thousands of readers sense his understanding of their own fears and faith. He coined the phrase "wounded healer," and out of his own suffering he became an agent of God to touch, bless, and heal thousands around the world.

In Nouwen's Voice

Henri Nouwen's writing revolves around a limited number of themes. Our self-rejection; God's love; our need for solitude, silence, and prayer; the imitation of Christ; the imperative of community; and ministry out of woundedness are some of them. By way of illustration, here are selected statements all taken from his insightful book *The Return of the Prodigal Son* [New York: Doubleday, 1992].

On the younger son: "Addiction" might be the best word to describe the lostness that so deeply penetrates contemporary society. Our addictions make us cling to what the world proclaims as the keys to self-fulfillment. As long as we live within the world's delusions, our addictions condemn us to futile quests in "the distant country" (p. 38f.).

Yes, I am leaving the foreign country. Yes, I am going home but I still live as though the God to whom I am returning demands an explanation. Belief in total, absolute forgiveness does not come easily (p. 47).

On the elder son: All my life I have harbored a strange curiosity for the disobedient life that I myself didn't dare to live, but which I saw

153

being lived by many around me. The obedient and dutiful life of which I am proud or for which I am praised feels, sometimes, like a burden that was laid on my shoulders (p. 65).

The father does not compare the two sons. He loves them both with a complete love and expresses that love according to their individual journeys. He sees with love the passion of his younger son, even when it is not regulated by obedience. With the same love, he sees the obedience of the elder son, even when it is not vitalized by passion (p. 76).

On the father: Rembrandt's painting and his own tragic life have offered me a context in which to discover that the final stage of the spiritual life is to so fully let go of all fear of the Father that it becomes possible to become like him. As long as the Father evokes fear, he remains an outsider and cannot dwell within me. But . . . my final vocation is indeed to become like the Father and to live out his divine compassion in my daily life. Though I am both the younger son and the elder son, I am not to remain them, but to become the Father (p. 114).

Perhaps the most radical statement Jesus ever made is: "Be compassionate as your Father is compassionate". . . . What I am called to make true is that whether I am the younger or the elder son, I am the son of my compassionate Father. I am an heir. . . . Indeed, as son and heir I am to become successor. . . . Being in the Father's house requires that I make the Father's life my own and become transformed in his image (p. 115f.).

AFTERWORD

Over the course of more than twenty centuries since the birth of Christ, the words of holy men and women have been spoken, remembered, transcribed, written down and preserved, in memory and on parchment, with pen and ink and word processors, and now even engraved for eternity in the cloud. In an era when the news cycle tends to be forty-eight hours or less, their words seem ancient, yet through the grace of God and the power of their testimony, they live on and breathe into us today.

As we have encountered in their stories, common themes of suffering and joy, isolation and misunderstanding, and both early death and long life, have threaded their way through their stories. These accounts are not hagiographies, idealized stories of saints, but instead, they aim to see both their flaws and their strengths, reminding us time and again that God uses those who are faithful, as "his strength is made perfect in weakness."

A word of explanation for the bibliography. There are many translations and printings of the words of our friends. Where Dr. Flora has been specific about his preferences or has quoted a source, these details have been noted. Otherwise, the author's name and title stand alone, and today's reader can follow those names through the wonders of the Internet to discover available copies, both in their original words and languages, and in more contemporary translations and paraphrases of their works. One helpful resource is published by Paulist Press in the series, *Classics of Western Spirituality*, which has gathered more than 130 volumes featuring spiritual writers through the centuries.

Henri Nouwen reflected, "It always strikes me how grateful people are for a good spiritual conversation, but also how hard it is to make such a conversation happen" [Seeds of Hope: A Henri Nouwen

155

Reader, (New York: Bantam Books, p. 63-64)]. We are grateful to Jerry Flora and his classic friends for leading the way.

JoAnn Streeter Shade

BIBLIOGRAPHY

Prepared by Judy Reber McLaughlin

Appleton, George, ed. *The Oxford Book of Prayer* (New York: Oxford University Press, 1985).

Armstrong, R. J. and I. C. Brady, eds. *Francis and Clare: The Complete Works. Classics of Western Spirituality* (London: Collins Liturgical Press, 1986).

Athanasius. *Life of Antony.*

Augustine of Hippo. *On the Trinity.*

———. *City of God.*

———. *Confessions of St. Augustine.*

———. *The Confessions of St. Augustine* Helms, Hal M. (Brewster, MA: Paraclete Press, 1986).

Beasley-Topliffe, Keith, ed. *Encounter with God's Love: Selected Writings of Julian of Norwich* (Nashville: Upper Room Books, 1998).

Bernard of Clairvaux. *On the Love of God.* (see Foster and Smith edition).

Bonhoeffer, Dietrich. *Love Letters from Cell 92* (1995).

———*The Cost of Discipleship,* trans. by R. H. Fuller (London: SCM Press, 2nd ed., 1959). This book is now published under the title, *Discipleship.*

———*Life Together,* trans. By John W. Doberstein (London: SCM Press, 1954)

———*Letters and Papers from Prison* (1951).

Brown, Raphael, trans. *The Little Flowers of Saint Francis* (New York: Doubleday, 1958).

Bunyan, John. *The Holy War.*

———. *The Life and Death of Mister Badman.*

———. *Grace Abounding to the Chief of Sinners.*

_____. *The New Pilgrim's Progress,* Markham, Judith E. ed. revised text (Grand Rapids: Discovery House Publishers, 1989).

Carmichael, Alexander. *Carmina Gadelica* (Edinburgh: Floris Books, 1992).

Chambers, Oswald. *My Utmost for His Highest* (London: Simpkin Marshall Ltd. 1927)).

Cunningham, Lawrence. *Thomas Merton: Spiritual Master* (New York: Paulist Press, 1992).

Davies, Oliver, ed. *Celtic Spirituality* in *Classics of Western Spirituality* (Paulist Press, 1999).

Davies, Oliver and Fiona Bowie. *Celtic Christian Spirituality* (Continuum, 1995).

DeWaal, Esther. *God Under My Roof.* (Brewster, MA: Paraclete Press, 1984).

_____*The Celtic Way of Prayer* (Doubleday, 1997).

Foster, Richard J. and James Bryan Smith, ed. *Devotional Classics: Selected Readings for Individuals and Groups* (HarperSanFrancisco, 1993).

Francis of Assisi. *Fioretti. The Little Flowers of St. Francis.*

_____. *The Canticle of Brother Sun.*

_____. *St. Francis of Assisi: Omnibus of Sources,* Habig, M.A., ed. 2nd ed. (London, SPCK, 1979).

_____. *St. Francis of Assisi: Omnibus of Sources,* ed. By M. A. Habig. 2nd ed. (London: SPCK, 1979).

Greene, Dana, ed. *Fragments from an Inner Life* (Harrisburg, PA: Morehouse Publishing, 1993).

Janz, Denis. *Three Reformation Catechisms: Catholic, Anabaptist, Lutheran* (New York: Edwin Mellen Press, 1982).

Job, Reuben P. and Norman Shawchuck, ed. *A Guide to Prayer for Ministers and Other Servants,* (Nashville: The Upper Room, 1983).

John of the Cross. *Living Flame of Love.*

_____*The Ascent of Mount Carmel.*

_____*The Dark Night.*

_____*The Spiritual Canticle.*

_____*The Living Flame of Love.*

Joyce, Timothy, O.S.B. *Celtic Christianity* (Orbis Press, 1998).

Julian of Norwich. *All Shall Be Well: Daily Readings from Julian of Norwich,* abridged and arranged by Sheila Upjohn (Harrisburg, PA: Morehouse Publishing, 1992).

Kelly, Richard. *Thomas Kelly: A Biography* (New York: Harper and Row Publishers, 1966).

Kelly, Thomas R. *A Testament of Devotion.* (HarperSanFrancisco, 1996).

_____.*The Eternal Promise* (New York: Harper and Row Publishers, 1966).

Lawrence of the Resurrection. *The Practice of the Presence of God* (1692).

_____. *The Practice of the Presence of God.* Edmonson, Robert J., trans. Christian Classics Living Library (Brewster, MA: Paraclete Press, rev. ed.,1983).

_____. *The Practice of the Presence of God* Helms, Hal M. trans. (Brewster, MA: Paraclete Press, 1984).

Lewis, C.S. *The Weight of Glory and Other Addresses* (HarperSanFrancisco, 2001).

_____*God in the Dock.*

_____*Letters to Malcolm: Chiefly on Prayer* (New York: Harcourt, Brace & World, 1963).

_____*Mere Christianity* (New York: the Macmillan Company, 1960).

_____*Till We Have Faces.*

_____*Surprised by Joy.*

_____*A Grief Observed.*

_____*The Chronicles of Narnia.*

_____Broadcast Talks: *Beyond Personality: or First Steps in the Doctrine of the Trinity* (1944).

Llewelyn, Robert, ed. *Daily Readings with Julian of Norwich, volume 1* (Springfield, IL: Templegate Publishers, 1980).

Luther, Martin. *Table Talk.*

_____*The Small Catechism.*

_____*The Bondage of the Will.*

_____*The Freedom of a Christian.*

_____*The Babylonian Captivity of the Church.*

_____*To the Christian Nobility of the German Nation.*

McCasland, David. *Oswald Chambers: Abandoned to God* (Our Daily Bread 1998).

Merton, Thomas. *The Asian Journal of Thomas Merton.*

_____*Contemplation in a World of Action.* (

_____*Contemplative Prayer.*

_____*Conjectures of a Guilty Bystander.*

_____*Raids on the Unspeakable.*

_____*The Way of Chuang Tzu.*

_____*New Seeds of Contemplation.*

_____*Disputed Questions.*

_____*The Wisdom of the Desert* (New York: New Directions Publishing Corporation, 1960).

_____*Thoughts in Solitude* (New York: Farrar, Straus and Giroux, 1958).

_____*No Man is an Island.*

_____*The Sign of Jonas.*

_____*The Seven Storey Mountain.*

Nouwen, Henri. *The Inner Voice of Love: A Journey Through Anguish to Freedom* (1996).

_____*The Return of the Prodigal Son: A Meditation on Fathers, Brothers, and Sons* (New York: Doubleday, 1992).

_____*The Road to Daybreak.*

_____*Gracias! A Latin American Journal.*

_____*The Way of the Heart: Desert Spirituality and Contemporary Ministry.*

_____*The Genesee Diary.*

_____*Reaching Out: The Three Movements of the Spiritual Life.*

_____*With Open Hands.*

_____*The Wounded Healer: Ministry in Contemporary Society.*

Nouwen, Henri and Yushi Nomura. *Wisdom from the Desert: Sayings from the Desert Fathers.*

Pooley, Roger and Philip Seddon, eds. *The Lord of the Journey: A Reader in Christian Spirituality* (London: Collins Liturgical Publications, 1986).

Slough, Rebecca, ed. *Hymnal: A Worship Book* (Scottsdale, PA: Mennonite Publishing House, 1992).

Smith, Hannah Whitall. *The Christian's Secret of a Happy Life.*

Talbot, John Michael with Steve Rabey. *The Lessons of St. Francis: How to Bring Simplicity and Spirituality into Your Daily Life* (New York: Penguin, 1997).

Teresa of Avila. *The Story of My Life.*

_____. *Interior Castle* Peers, E. Allison, trans. and ed. (Image Books New York: Doubleday, 1989).

The United Methodist Hymnal (Nashville: The United Methodist Publishing House, 1989).

Thomas à Kempis. *The Imitation of Christ.*

_____. *The Imitation of Christ: A Timeless Classic for Contemporary Readers.* Creasy, William C., trans. (Notre Dame, IN: Ave Maria Press, 1989).

Underhill, Evelyn, *Mysticism: A Study of the Nature and Development of Spiritual Consciousness.*

_____*The House of the Soul and Concerning the Inner Life* (Minneapolis: Seabury Press, n.d.).

_____*Worship.*

_____*What Is the Spiritual Life* in *The Spiritual Life* (London: Hodder and Stoughton, 1937).

_____. *Abba*

_____. *The Golden Sequence*

_____. *The House of the Soul*

_____. *Concerning the Inner Life*

Wesley, Charles. Hymns:
A Charge to Keep I Have
And Can It Be that I Should Gain?
Christ the Lord is Risen Today
Hark! The Herald Angels Sing
Jesus, Lover of My Soul
Love Divine, All Loves Excelling
Rejoice, the Lord is King

Soldiers of Christ, Arise

Ye Servants of God, Your Master Proclaim

Wesley, John. *A Collection of Hymns for the Use of . . . Methodists.*

———. *John Wesley's Covenant Service* (Nashville: Discipleship Resources, n.d.).

Woods, Richard J. *Christian Spirituality: God's Presence through the Ages* (Maryknoll, NY: Orbis Books, rev. ed., 2006).

ABOUT THE AUTHOR

Since the age of eight when he first walked his church's red-carpeted aisle for salvation, Jerry Flora has been a Jesus follower. Answering a call to ministry, he trained at the former Ashland College and Seminary. He served as a pastor first in a small village in Indiana and then in an urban neighborhood in Washington, D.C. Graduate degrees from Fuller Seminary and The Southern Baptist Theological Seminary readied him for a teaching career. He returned to Ashland Seminary where he taught for thirty years. At retirement in 2002 Dr. Flora was named Professor Emeritus of Theology and Spiritual Formation.

Although he has lived from coast to coast, he is a Hoosier by birth and a Buckeye by adoption. Along the way he has been a janitor, caddy, lawn-care worker, choir director and retreat speaker. He was co-founder of the LifeSpring School of Spiritual Formation and its co-director for ten years. From 1995 to 2008 he was a guest instructor at Pennsylvania's Kairos School of Spiritual Formation. He has also served as national vice-president and newsletter editor for the Disciplined Order of Christ. He is the author of *The Message of Faith*, *Into Your Hands: Memoir and Witness*, and *Amen: Short Prayers for Any Time*.

Dr. Flora and his wife Julie have been married almost seventy years. They have two daughters, Janet and Ann, two grandchildren, Vanessa and Matthew, and two great-grandchildren, Maddox and Isabella. A soul-friend to many, he relishes family and friends, reading and music, sunrise and sunset.

ABOUT THE LITERARY MIDWIVES

In the spirit of the Old Testament midwives, Shiphrah and Puah (see Exodus 1), Judy and JoAnn joyfully served as literary midwives for the birth of this volume.

Dr. Judith Reber McLaughlin received a Master of Arts in Pastoral Counseling from Ashland Theological Seminary, a second Master's in Spiritual Formation and a Ph.D. in Formative Spirituality from Duquesne University in Pittsburgh. She served as a mental health professional at Emerge Ministries and an adjunct instructor at Ashland Seminary.

Judy enjoys activities in her local faith community where she is a Prayer Group member and serves as a Reader in worship services. Daily grateful for being able to nurture friendships with family and friends, she especially loves surprise visits from her children and their families and celebrates the progress of her seven "Grands" who are making the world a better place to live.

Dr. JoAnn Streeter Shade retired in 2012 from full-time ministry in the Salvation Army, where her last assignment was the development of the Ray and Joan Kroc Corps Community Center in Ashland, OH. She is the author of more than twenty books on topics such as spiritual growth (The Heartwork of Hope, The God Gallery), sexual abuse (Rapha's Touch), marriage (The Guerilla and the Green Beret), retirement (To Be Continued . . . Women, Ministry and Retirement), and biblical women (The Other Woman, Ezer Strong, and The House of Women).

She is married to Larry, is the mother of three adult sons, Greg, Drew and Dan, and two beloved daughters-in-law (Lauren and Becky), and is Nana to five grandchildren. With an M.A. in pastoral counseling and a D.Min. in the Women in Prophetic Leadership track from Ashland Theological Seminary, she combines her academic training with a writer's eye, a pastor's heart and a grandmother's joy.

OTHER BOOKS BY JERRY FLORA

Amen: Short Prayers for Any Time
Into Your Hands: Memoir and Witness
The Journey is Our Home: Married Sixty Years
(with Julie Flora)
The Message of Faith

Made in the USA
Columbia, SC
27 November 2024

47235944R00096